Security Technologies for Law Enforcement Agencies

In a rapidly evolving world where technology is increasingly integrated into our daily lives, security has become a top priority for individuals, organizations, and governments. *Security Technologies for Law Enforcement Agencies* offers a comprehensive examination of the tools, systems, and concepts that form the foundation of modern security infrastructures.

This extensive guide takes readers on a journey from fundamental concepts to the latest innovations. It clearly outlines the role of security, technology, and research and development (R&D) in advancing security capabilities. This book also emphasizes the delicate balance between public safety and individual privacy.

Readers will discover how technologies such as night vision cameras, thermal imaging, and unmanned aerial vehicles (UAVs) are revolutionizing urban security and crime prevention. From facial recognition systems to advanced biometric authentication, this book provides striking insights into how controlled access technologies protect sensitive spaces.

Providing an in-depth look at the essential role of hardware and software in security, this book covers global positioning systems (GPS), optical and laser technologies, and the latest developments in 5G communications. It also delves into software-driven identity verification systems, such as facial recognition and license plate identification, illustrating their impact on public safety and legal compliance.

Security Technologies for Law Enforcement Agencies explores future technological trends and revolutionary developments from NATO's perspective. With this forward-looking approach, security professionals, policymakers, researchers, and enthusiasts are equipped with the knowledge needed to navigate the rapidly shifting landscape of electronic security.

Whether you are a security professional, an academic, or a curious reader eager to understand the systems shaping our world, this book serves as an essential resource. It brings clarity to the complexities of modern security, inspiring readers to engage with the technologies that protect our communities and drive societal progress.

Cyber Shorts Series

Discover concise and focused books on specific cybersecurity topics with Cyber Shorts. This book series is designed for students, professionals, and enthusiasts seeking to explore specialized areas within cybersecurity. From blockchain to zero-day to ethical hacking, each book provides real-world examples and practical insights.

For more information about this series, please visit: www.routledge.com/Cyber-Shorts/book-series/CYBSH

Security Technologies for Law Enforcement Agencies

Kazım Duraklar

CRC Press
Taylor & Francis Group
Boca Raton London New York

CRC Press is an imprint of the
Taylor & Francis Group, an **informa** business

Designed cover image: Shutterstock Image ID 2509710595

First edition published 2025
by CRC Press
2385 NW Executive Center Drive, Suite 320, Boca Raton FL 33431

and by CRC Press
4 Park Square, Milton Park, Abingdon, Oxon, OX14 4RN

CRC Press is an imprint of Taylor & Francis Group, LLC

ISBN: 9781032980324 (hbk)
ISBN: 9781032981796 (pbk)
ISBN: 9781003597445 (ebk)

DOI: 10.1201/9781003597445

Typeset in Sabon
by Deanta Global Publishing Services, Chennai, India

Contents

Preface

In an era defined by rapid technological advancements and escalating security concerns, electronic security technologies have emerged as indispensable tools for safeguarding individuals, communities, and nations. This book embarks on a comprehensive exploration of these technologies, delving into their fundamental principles, diverse applications, and far-reaching implications for the future.

From the surveillance systems that monitor our cities to the biometric scanners that guard our buildings, electronic security technologies are ubiquitous in our daily lives. Yet, their underlying mechanisms, capabilities, and ethical considerations often remain shrouded in complexity. This book aims to demystify this intricate landscape, providing a clear and accessible guide to the world of electronic security.

We begin by establishing a foundational understanding of key concepts, including security, technology, and technological systems (Chapter 1). We then delve into the critical role of research and development in driving innovation, emphasizing the importance of domestic capabilities and national security interests. The ethical dimensions of security technologies are also examined, highlighting the delicate balance between safety and privacy.

This book then embarks on a detailed exploration of electronically based reconnaissance, surveillance, and detection systems, shedding light on their pivotal role in urban security management (Chapter 2). We dissect the inner workings of basic and high-resolution imaging systems, as well as the cutting-edge technologies of night vision and thermal cameras.

Next, we turn our attention to electronically based controlled access systems (Chapter 3), which are essential for safeguarding buildings and facilities. We investigate top search systems, authentication mechanisms, and alarm systems, providing insights into their effectiveness and potential vulnerabilities.

"Software-Based Personal Identity Verification Technologies" (Chapter 4) addresses the legal frameworks governing personal identity verification. It explores innovative methods such as personal identity inquiry via radio tablets, face recognition applications, and number plate identification systems.

These technologies are increasingly important for verifying identities and enhancing security in both public and private sectors.

"Hardware-Based Communication Technologies" (Chapter 5) explores the various communication systems essential for security operations. It covers narrowband and broadband systems, stringed systems, and mixing and blending systems, which are vital for ensuring secure and reliable communication in various security scenarios.

This book then shifts its focus to critical embedded system-based technologies (Chapter 6), such as global positioning system (GPS), optical and laser systems, and 5G communication technologies. These technologies play a crucial role in various domains, from navigation and communication to infrastructure management and data collection.

Finally, we venture into the realm of advanced technologies that are poised to revolutionize the field of electronic security. We also gaze into the future, speculating on the next wave of technological advancements and their implications for security.

In conclusion, this book offers a comprehensive and accessible overview of electronic security technologies, catering to a diverse audience, including security professionals, policymakers, researchers, and anyone with an interest in the evolving landscape of security in the digital age. By understanding the intricacies of these technologies, we can harness their potential to create a safer and more secure world for all.

About the Author

Kazım Duraklar is an academic with a PhD in Electrical and Electronics Engineering from the Graduate School of Natural Sciences at Gazi University, Ankara, Türkiye. He completed his undergraduate studies in Electrical and Electronics Engineering as well as in Electronics Education, followed by a master's degree in Computer Engineering from Karabük University, Karabük, Türkiye.

Starting his academic career in 2008, Duraklar has taken on teaching and managerial roles in fields such as industrial automation, power electronics, cybersecurity technologies, IoT-based systems, and security technologies. Currently serving as a lecturer at the Gendarmerie and Coast Guard Academy, he has participated in numerous national and international projects, making significant contributions, particularly in solar energy and Industry 4.0 applications.

Duraklar has published articles, book chapters, and scientific studies in various journals. He also plays an active role as a project coordinator, board member, and participant in social responsibility initiatives. He is recognized as an academic who develops innovative approaches in engineering and technology.

Chapter 1

Basic concepts in electronic-based security technologies

1.1 DEFINITIONS: SECURITY, TECHNOLOGY, AND TECHNOLOGICAL SYSTEMS

Security literally refers to the measures and practices taken to protect any person, object, or system from harmful effects. In general terms, security refers to measures designed to reduce risks, protect against threats, and prevent unwanted events (Schneier, 2004). Before analyzing the meaning of the word security, it would be more useful to understand its essence. In this sense, imagine a caveman is keeping watch to warn everyone in advance in case of unexpected danger, protecting his cave with a spear, and ensuring that the people in the cave know what to do in a dangerous situation. From this point of view, seeing the cave as the physical element of security, the people in the cave as the human and process elements, the spear in the hand as the technical element, the awareness of the danger as the information element, the exchange of news between cave individuals as the communication element, and the cave leader as the management element reveals seven important basic elements of security. The absence of any of these elements indicates that the provision of safety will be negatively affected. The basic elements of security are presented in Figure 1.1.

When the concept of security is considered in terms of individuals in society, it is briefly defined as the protection of vital interests in a sovereign area. This definition also reveals the impact of the concept of territoriality. With rapidly increasing globalization, this territoriality has been questioned, and the distinction between internal and external security, traditionally seen as the responsibility of different institutions, has begun to disappear. Globalization has led to the intertwining of internal and external problems, causing states to operate in an area where internal and external security problems intersect (Baldwin, 1997). For example, while the interaction between internal and external security has increased with the impact of globalization, the dividing line between law enforcement and armed forces has become blurred. In this framework, the legal borders of the state have a symbolic meaning. The blurring of the dividing line between internal and external borders of security provides an analytical

DOI: 10.1201/9781003597445-1

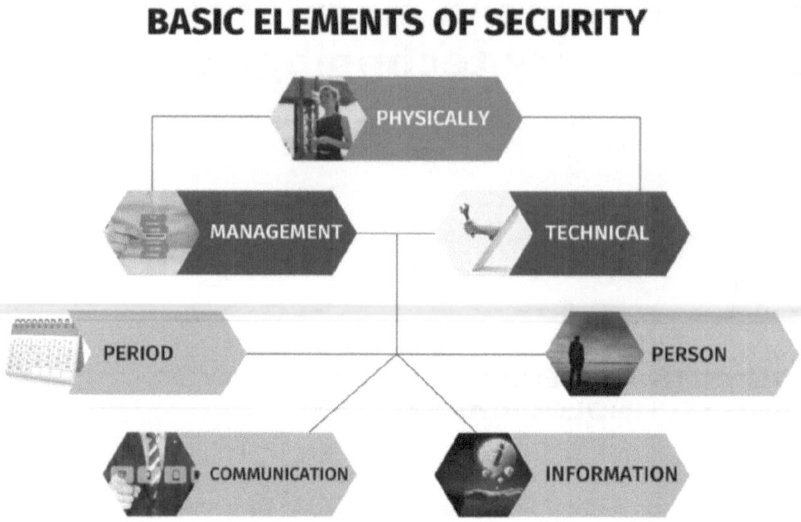

BASIC ELEMENTS OF SECURITY

Figure 1.1 Basic elements of security

entry point for understanding the relationship between security and globalization (Baldwin, 1997).

The term technology briefly refers to the production of practical applications such as machines and devices using scientific knowledge. In general, technology covers all kinds of practical knowledge and applications developed and used by humans, such as tools, machines, devices, and systems. Technology products and applications are used to facilitate human life, solve problems, create new opportunities, and make work more efficient (Jasanoff, 2006). Computers, communication networks, robots, artificial intelligence, automation, and many other areas are examples of technology, but technology is constantly developing and advancing, affecting many aspects of our lives with new discoveries and innovations. Key elements of technology definition are presented in Figure 1.2.

Law enforcement agencies that fight against crime scenes and conflict zones actively use technology and constantly follow technological developments. As law enforcement agencies, especially the vital importance of information sharing makes it mandatory for law enforcement agencies to specialize in technological systems. This reliance on technology in law enforcement is increasingly critical for effective crime prevention and security operations (Berghel, 2017). Hardware and software elements work together to form an integrated technological system. Hardware refers to the physical components of a computer or an electronic system. These components include parts such as processor, memory, hard disk, motherboard, screen, and keyboard (Stallings, 2015). Hardware processes data, executes commands, and performs various functions. Software is the set of

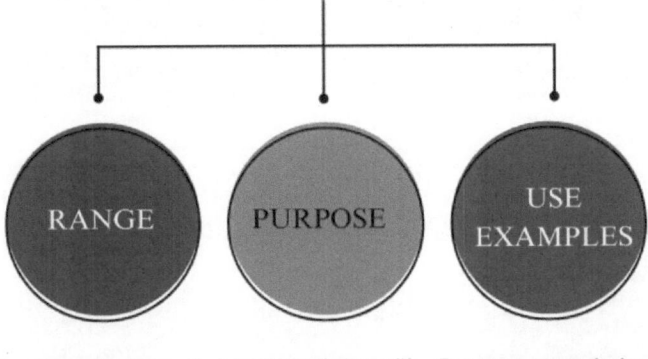

TECHNOLOGY

Technology refers to the combination of scientific knowledge and practical applications.
Technology constantly evolves and advances, affecting many aspects of our lives with new discoveries and innovations.

RANGE — It covers all kinds of practical knowledge and applications developed and used by humans, such as tools, machines, devices and systems.

PURPOSE — It is used to make human life easier, solve problems, create new opportunities and make work more efficient.

USE EXAMPLES — Computers, communication networks, robots, artificial intelligence, automation and many other fields are examples of technology.

Figure 1.2 Key elements of technology definition

programs and instructions that make a computer or an electronic system work. Software performs certain tasks by running on hardware. These tasks can be a variety of software, such as operating systems, application software, drivers, and simulations (Tanenbaum & Wetherall, 2011). Software helps users to perform their functions and controls the hardware. Hardware represents the power and capabilities provided by physical components, while software uses that hardware to perform operations and produce results. A harmonious combination of hardware and software ensures that a system is effective, efficient, and performs the desired tasks. This seamless integration of software and hardware systems is crucial in ensuring optimal performance in law enforcement operations (Gupta & Gupta, 2018). Examples of the main components of technological systems are presented in Figure 1.3.

From drones in the sky to criminal analysis in laboratories, many technological systems are used by law enforcement agencies. In this context, the dimensions of security are constantly evolving due to rapid advancements in technology (Jones & Newburn, 2013). The relationship between law enforcement units and technology is closely associated with the technological opportunities and capabilities that these units can utilize. Technological advancements, such as artificial intelligence and big data,

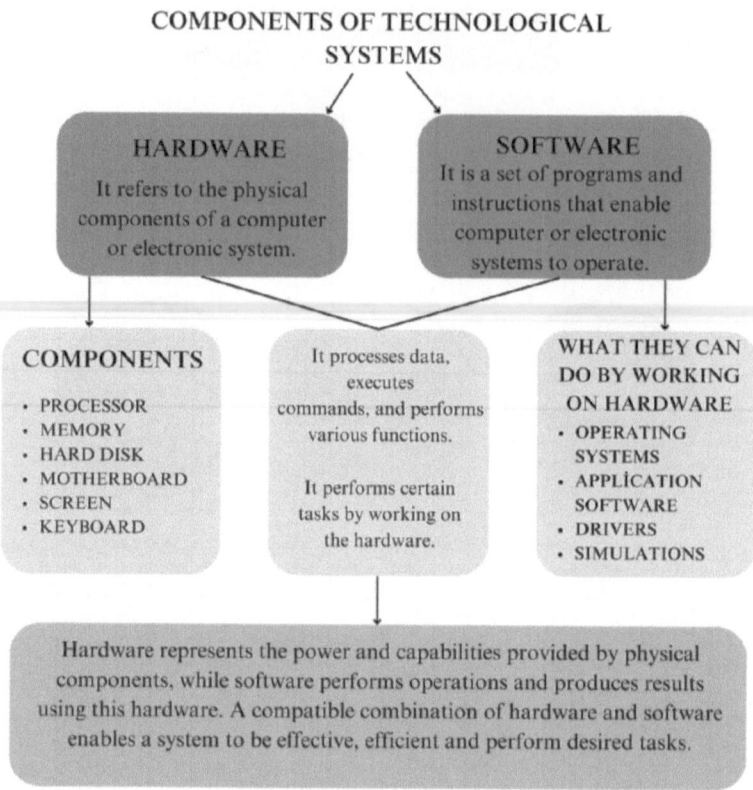

COMPONENTS OF TECHNOLOGICAL SYSTEMS

HARDWARE

It refers to the physical components of a computer or electronic system.

SOFTWARE

It is a set of programs and instructions that enable computer or electronic systems to operate.

COMPONENTS

- PROCESSOR
- MEMORY
- HARD DISK
- MOTHERBOARD
- SCREEN
- KEYBOARD

It processes data, executes commands, and performs various functions.

It performs certain tasks by working on the hardware.

WHAT THEY CAN DO BY WORKING ON HARDWARE

- OPERATING SYSTEMS
- APPLICATION SOFTWARE
- DRIVERS
- SIMULATIONS

Hardware represents the power and capabilities provided by physical components, while software performs operations and produces results using this hardware. A compatible combination of hardware and software enables a system to be effective, efficient and perform desired tasks.

Figure 1.3 Components of technological systems

are reshaping the strategies of law enforcement agencies (Chen et al., 2004). Thus, it is imperative to determine what the technological needs are and which innovations should be prioritized in order for law enforcement agencies to work effectively and efficiently in the coming years (Bueermann, 2012).

The stage of defining the basic ideas, objectives, and features at the beginning of the development process of a technology or product is called conceptualization in technology. This stage involves creating an understanding of the needs, goals, and use cases of a new product, service, or technology (Rogers, 2003). The stages of concept definition are presented in Figure 1.4.

The conceptualization phase is crucial to the success of a project. This stage forms the cornerstone that guides future research, design, development, and marketing processes. Effective conceptualization ensures that a clear understanding of the goals and objectives is established early on, which is vital for the later stages of a project (Cooper, 2014). The criteria system used to determine the stages and maturity level of the development

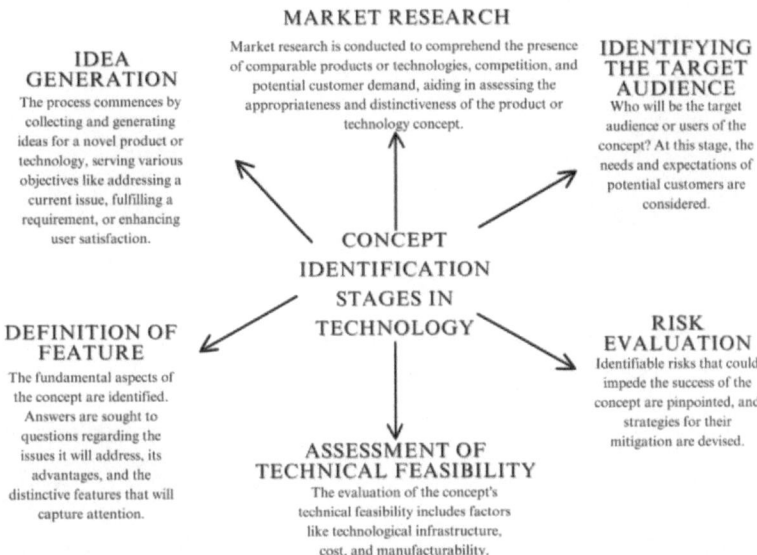

Figure 1.4 Concept identification stages in technology

process of a technology from scientific method to commercial product is called technology readiness level (TRL). This concept is widely used, especially in research and development projects and technology transfer (Mankins, 2009). The TRL was developed by the US National Aeronautics and Space Administration (NASA) in the 1980s and has since been adopted by other organizations and industries for technology assessment and management (Sauser et al., 2006). The TRL uses a scale of nine stages from one to nine, where each stage represents a higher level of technological maturity, from initial basic research to final commercial deployment. This scale is presented in Figure 1.5.

TRL is seen as an important tool for monitoring the development stages of a technology and measuring progress. It is especially used to determine the maturity level of new technologies before they are introduced to the market and to mitigate risks.

1.2 RESEARCH AND DEVELOPMENT

Innovation is the application of changes or new ideas to improve the status quo or create something new. Innovation refers to the creation of new methods, products, processes, or services or the improvement of existing ones (Schilling, 2017). Innovation often takes place through the use of knowledge and technology. Scientific and technological advances, in particular, provide a strong foundation for innovation, helping organizations and

TRL 1:
FUNDAMENTAL
SCIENTIFIC RESEARCH

Understanding and
familiarity with concepts,
theories, or fundamental
principles.

TRL 2:
TECHNOLOGICAL
FORMULATION

The stage where
technological goals are
defined and initial
experimental evidence
based on fundamental
research findings is
discovered.

LEVELS OF TECHNOLOGICAL READINESS

TRL 3:
ANALYTICAL AND
EMPIRICAL EVIDENCE

Fundamental technological
concepts established and
verified in a laboratory
setting.

TRL 8:
AUTHENTIC
SYSTEM
VALIDATION

TRL 9:
ACTUAL SYSTEM IN A
BUSINESS SETTING

Phase of
extensive testing
with a fully
operational and
ready system.

The stage of full
deployment and
operation of technology
in a live business setting.

TRL 4:
TECHNOLOGY
VALIDATION

The stage of verifying
critical subsystem
components in the
laboratory environment.

TRL 7:
PROTOTYPING
IN A
CORPORATE
SETTING

TRL 6:
DEMONSTRATION OF A
PROTOTYPE SYSTEM

TRL 5:
PROTOTYPE SYSTEM
TESTING.

The phase of
testing the
prototype under
actual operating
conditions.

The phase during which
the prototype undergoes
testing under actual work
conditions in suitable
simulated environments.

The phase during which
the prototype undergoes
testing at full scale in a
laboratory setting and
relevant simulated
environments.

Figure 1.5 Technology readiness level scales

industries gain competitive advantage, increase productivity, and ensure customer satisfaction while promoting societal progress (Tidd & Bessant, 2020). Innovation can be applied in various fields, including technology, health, education, business, agriculture, energy, transportation, and many more. This process typically involves creativity, risk-taking, and entrepreneurship, encouraging the creation of new opportunities and solutions (Drucker, 2002).

Research and development (R&D) stages are key elements in driving innovation. Research is defined as contributing to existing knowledge or using scientific methods to solve specific problems (Creswell, 2014). It is a systematic and disciplined process aimed at gathering information, discovering facts, solving problems, and generating new knowledge. The research process includes steps such as data collection, analysis, interpretation of results, and the reporting of findings. Scientific methods are typically used to produce solid, evidence-based, and objective results. Research is applied across many disciplines, including academic, medical, social science, and market research, all contributing to the advancement of knowledge and societal progress (Bhattacherjee, 2012).

Development is the practical application of research findings to create useful substances, tools, products, systems, or services, or to improve existing ones. It is a process aimed at enhancing the effectiveness, efficiency, or utility of products and services (Wheelwright & Clark, 1992). Through continuous innovation, quality improvement, and strategic decision-making, the development process ensures sustained progress and competitive advantage in the marketplace. The picture representing the research is presented in Figure 1.6.

Figure 1.6 **Research**

Development refers to the use of the results of basic and applied research to create various useful substances, tools, products, systems, and production methods or to enhance existing ones. Development is the process or activity of making something better, advancing, or enlarging it. It is usually carried out to make progress towards a specific goal or purpose. Development aims to make a product, service, process, system, or idea more effective, efficient, or useful by making improvements to it. The development process may involve research, planning, design, implementation, testing, and evaluation. Needs can be analyzed, innovative ideas generated, resources allocated, and strategic decisions made. The process is often iterative and aims to make progress continuously. Development is applied in many fields. For example, development activities are carried out in different areas such as software development, product development, business process development, and organizational development. The development process aims to achieve goals such as innovation, quality improvement, productivity improvement, and customer satisfaction. The picture regarding the development process is presented in Figure 1.7.

Figure 1.7 Development process

R&D is a combined abbreviation of the words "Research" and "Development". R&D refers to disciplined efforts to discover new knowledge and technologies, deepen existing knowledge, and develop applicable products, processes, or services. Research and development activities are usually carried out in scientific and technological fields. These studies may include processes such as discovering new ideas, conducting basic research, designing and developing new products, improving processes, using new technologies, and conducting innovation activities. The purpose of Research and development activities is to advance knowledge and technology, gain a competitive advantage, encourage innovation, and support the emergence of new products, services, or processes. R&D activities can be carried out by academic institutions, private sector companies, government agencies, and other research centers. These studies usually require a high level of scientific and technical expertise and involve the use of advanced research methods and technologies. In general, technopolis and incubation centers are the centers of R&D activities. Types of units conducting R&D activities are presented in Figure 1.8.

Technopolises are special zones that bring together universities and research institutions with industry and the business world to support scientific research, development, and innovation activities. They aim to transform academic knowledge and technology into commercial products and services by encouraging university-industry cooperation. Technopolises are usually managed by the private or public sector and located near university campuses. Researchers, academics, and companies can conduct scientific research, develop technological projects, and offer innovative products or solutions. Technopolises can also host incubation centers that support entrepreneurs as well as companies that are usually focused on R&D and innovation. Incubation centers are usually places where entrepreneurs and start-up companies receive support and guidance to bring their business ideas to life. They provide an ideal environment for the "incubation

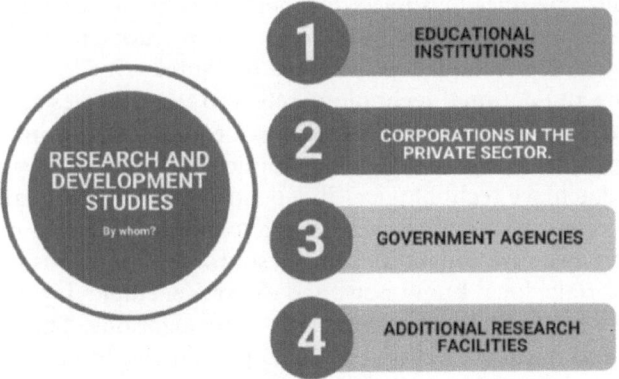

Figure 1.8 Types of units conducting R&D activities

period", a process where innovative business ideas are developed, tested, and brought to market. Incubators can operate as part of technopolises or universities or can be established independently. In incubators, entrepreneurs can develop their businesses by benefiting from mentoring, training, business planning, financing, marketing support, and infrastructure services. This process provides important support to help new ideas and companies get off the ground. By encouraging innovation, both structures enable the commercialization of new technologies and business ideas and contribute to economic growth. Technopolises focus on larger-scale R&D and innovation projects, while incubators typically focus on the needs of start-up entrepreneurs.

1.3 THE IMPORTANCE OF DOMESTIC AND NATIONALITY IN TECHNOLOGY

The terms "indigenous" and "national" are often used to refer to something that is unique to a country or community, produced or developed from local sources. The term indigenous refers to something produced or developed within a country's own territory or borders. Phrases such as domestic production or domestic technology refer to production or technology that is based in a country and utilizes local resources or domestic labor. The term national refers to something that represents the sovereignty and national interests of a country or is based on the shared values of a society. Phrases such as national product, national security, and national identity refer to things that reflect the values, interests, or independence of a country or society. These terms are used to promote local economic development, ensure technological independence, support sectors of strategic importance for national security, and emphasize the utilization of local resources. They can also refer to the development of local capabilities and the preservation of national identity and culture. However, the terms indigenous and national can sometimes be subject to political, economic, or social debates and be subject to different interpretations. The picture examples of domestic and national technology are presented in Figure 1.9.

Indigenous and national technology refers to technologies that a country or society produces or develops using its own resources. This aims to reduce external dependence, support local economic development, ensure national security, and achieve technological independence. Indigenous and national technology refers to technologies that a country develops or produces using its own in-house capabilities and resources. This means using locally sourced materials, local know-how, and expertise; employing a local workforce; and contributing local companies or organizations. The objectives of indigenous and national technology include reducing foreign dependence, strengthening the local economy, increasing the competitiveness of local companies, creating jobs, and developing local capabilities. It is also an important objective to ensure the use of indigenous and secure technologies

Figure 1.9 Examples of domestic and national technology

in sectors of strategic importance for national security. Domestic and national technology promotes innovation, supports technological progress, and ensures social development by relying on the country's own resources. These concepts aim to protect a country's technological independence and national interests.

In this context, our country launched the National Technology Move program in 2020. Its aim is to increase the country's technological independence, encourage the development of domestic and national technologies, and strengthen national interests in the field of science and technology. The main objectives of the National Technology Move include improving R&D and innovation capacity, increasing domestic production, becoming a country that can export high-tech products, producing technologies of strategic importance for national security, and focusing on new-generation technologies. Within the scope of this move, the private sector, universities, and public institutions work in cooperation and are supported for the development and dissemination of domestic technologies. The program focuses on strategic sectors such as defense, health, energy, agriculture, space, software, and information technologies. The National Technology Move is an important step towards Turkey's goal of becoming a technologically strong country and aims to contribute to the country's economic and scientific progress by supporting domestic production and innovation. It aims to strengthen the national technology ecosystem, train qualified manpower, and promote a technology-based economy.

1.4 TECHNOLOGY AND ETHICS

The concept of applied ethics has emerged with the idea that solutions can be found using current ethical approaches to the problems that arise with technology. Applied ethics, which tries to analyze the problems frequently encountered in private life as a result of technology as a moral and philosophical evaluation, is now divided into branches such as medical ethics, legal ethics, robot ethics, and environmental ethics. Applied ethics tries to create ideas about what to do in order to find solutions to the problems in society or to find concrete solutions.

The relationship between technology and ethics is concerned with the ethical issues and values that arise in the development, use, and dissemination of technology. Technology is a force that greatly affects societies and human life, and ethics helps to assess and guide these impacts of technology. The development and use of technology raises a variety of ethical issues. Ethical questions such as how to use technology, for whose benefit or harm, personal privacy, and data security are important topics of debate in the field of technology. The relationship between technology and ethics is presented in Figure 1.10.

Here are some important points to elaborate on the relationship between technology and ethics:

Artificial Intelligence and Ethics: Advanced technologies such as artificial intelligence play an important role, especially in terms of ethical issues. Ethical issues such as the biases of algorithms, the responsibility of autonomous systems, and the impact of artificial intelligence on human rights are important points of discussion in the field of technology.

Technological Responsibility: Technology developers, users, and stakeholders bear responsibility for the ethical use and positive outcomes of technology. The potential ethical implications of technological products and services should be considered and managed.

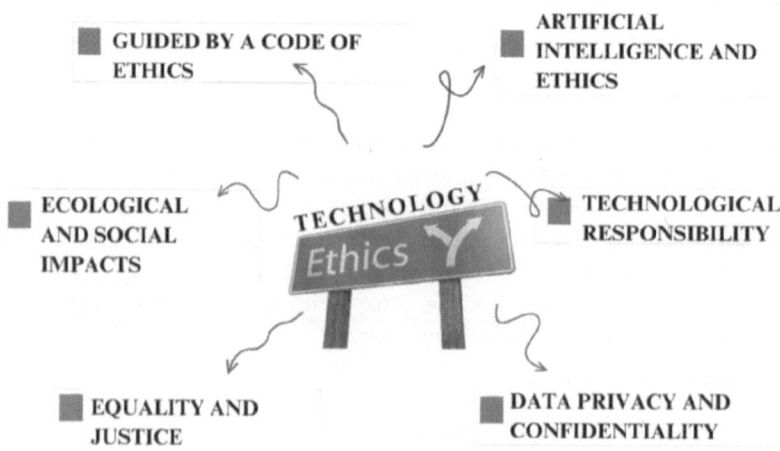

Figure 1.10 The relationship between technology and ethics

Data Privacy and Confidentiality: Data obtained through the use of technology raises concerns about the privacy and confidentiality of individuals. Ethical guidelines require sensitivity to the collection, storage, and sharing of this data.

Equality and Justice: Technology can increase or decrease inequalities and injustices in society. What is ethically important is to ensure that the benefits of technology are fairly distributed and accessible to all.

Ecological and Social Impacts: Technology has environmental and social impacts. Ethics assesses the impacts of technology on the environment and society and considers sustainability and societal well-being.

Guided by a Code of Ethics: Ethical codes and values are often considered to guide the development and use of technology. Ethical codes aim to ensure that technology is used in a fair and safe way that benefits people and society.

The relationship between technology and ethics aims to ensure that technology development is guided by societal values and ethics, and that it is used for the benefit of people. Therefore, those working in the field of technology, developers and users, should manage technology responsibly, taking into account ethical issues.

1.5 SECURITY TECHNOLOGIES AND PUBLIC SAFETY

In general terms, security constitutes a broad framework that includes physical security, personnel security, communication security, network security, and information security. In this framework, security technologies refer to technological solutions used to provide protection against harmful effects. These solutions can be used in the areas of physical, digital, or personal security. For example, security cameras, alarm systems, and access control systems can be given as examples of physical security technologies, while information security can be provided by using digital security technologies such as encryption, firewalls, and antivirus software. Security technologies are used to reduce risks, detect threats, protect against attacks, and prevent vulnerabilities. Constantly evolving technology leads to more advanced and effective security technologies to deal with new security threats. Security technologies are often interoperable and can be combined to create a holistic security solution.

Security technologies used in conflict environments and crime scenes help law enforcement agencies to conduct security operations more effectively and efficiently. These technologies aim to enhance both the security of security forces and public safety. Some key points on the importance of security technologies are presented in Figure 1.11.

Increased Surveillance and Monitoring: In conflict environments and crime scenes, security technologies enable increased surveillance and monitoring. With technologies such as camera systems, sensors, and drones, law

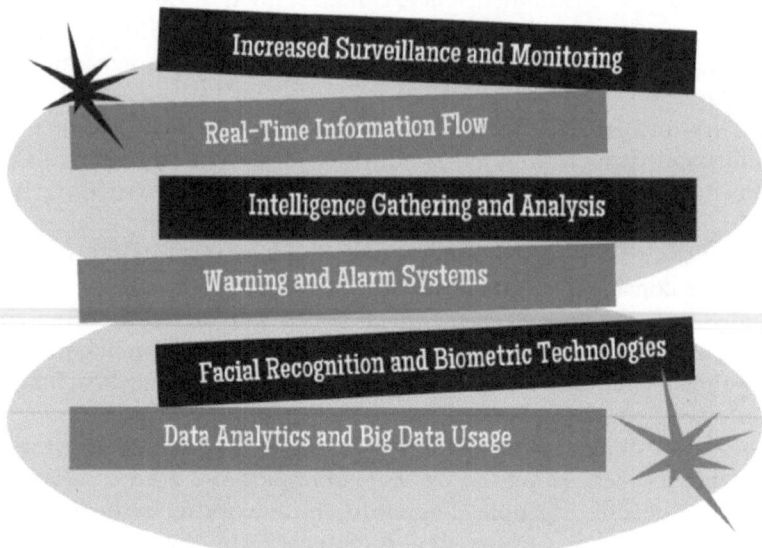

Figure 1.11 Some key points on the importance of security technologies

enforcement can better observe the area and detect security-related situations faster.

Real-time Information Flow: Security technologies increase the flow of information in real time. This helps law enforcement respond faster to incidents, respond more effectively to emergencies, and better understand security situations.

Intelligence Collection and Analysis: In conflict environments and crime scenes, security technologies enhance intelligence collection and analysis processes. This is important for identifying crime patterns, tracking the activities of criminals, and improving crime-fighting strategies.

Warning and Alarm Systems: Security technologies are equipped with warning and alarm systems. These systems detect potential threats at an early stage and direct security forces to respond quickly to incidents.

Facial Recognition and Biometric Technologies: Such technologies can be effective in recognizing and tracking criminals. Law enforcement can use biometric technologies, such as facial recognition and fingerprint scanning, to identify security threats and prevent potential crimes.

Data Analytics and Big Data Utilization: Security technologies can work more efficiently through the use of data analytics and big data. This helps analyze crime patterns and trends and better manage security measures.

Security technologies strengthen the security operations of law enforcement agencies and increase effectiveness in the fight against crime. By acting faster, more accurately, and more proactively, law enforcement agencies have a significant advantage in conflict environments and crime scenes to ensure public safety and protect the well-being of society. However, the effective use of these technologies requires sensitivity in protecting the confidentiality and lawfulness of data.

Law enforcement agencies utilize a variety of security technologies to ensure security and public order.

Surveillance Cameras: Cameras help law enforcement officers monitor public areas and criminal activity. In addition to helping prevent crime, these cameras are also used to collect evidence in cases where crimes have been committed.

Radio Communication Systems: Radio systems are used for communication between law enforcement agencies. These systems facilitate instant communication during emergencies, operations, and daily tasks.

Global Positioning System (GPS) Tracking Systems: Vehicle tracking systems help law enforcement agencies track and direct their vehicles and personnel. These systems are used to ensure rapid response and coordination.

Databases and Information Systems: Law enforcement agencies use databases and information systems to keep records of offenders and incidents. These systems are used in the fight against crime for purposes such as analyzing data, identifying relationships between incidents, and identifying crime patterns.

Authentication Technologies: Biometric technologies such as fingerprinting, retinal scanning, or facial recognition help law enforcement agencies to verify the identity of individuals. These are used to identify criminal suspects and fight crime.

Research and Investigation Tools: Law enforcement agencies use specialized investigative tools to collect and analyze evidence at crime scenes. For example, fingerprint collection equipment, chemical analyzers, and other technical equipment are used for this purpose.

Surveillance Camera Technologies: The process by which the principles of surveillance gained legitimacy and a position that was demanded by large segments of society was influenced by the widespread idea that the need for security around the world had increased even more after the end of the Cold War, which had a global impact, and the occurrence of situations that could be considered as turning points. Surveillance camera technologies are advancing rapidly.

Analog Cameras: Analog cameras capture and record images using conventional video signals. These cameras are commonly used in closed-circuit television (CCTV) systems. Analog cameras generally have lower image quality and offer limited resolution.

IP Cameras: Internet protocol (IP) cameras are cameras that transmit digital images directly over a network. These cameras offer high resolution, remote access, and more customization options. Because they are networked, IP cameras can support features such as remote access, monitoring, and recording.

Wireless Cameras: Wireless cameras are cameras that transmit images wirelessly. This type of camera eliminates the need to lay cables and allows for flexible placement. Wireless cameras typically use Wi-Fi or other wireless communication protocols.

PTZ Cameras: Pan-tilt-zoom (PTZ) cameras are zoom cameras that can move horizontally and vertically. These cameras can be managed remotely and allow operators to adjust the angle of view. PTZ cameras are used to monitor a wide area and zoom in to see details.

Thermal Cameras: Thermal cameras are powered by the heat energy emitted by objects. These cameras operate in the invisible light spectrum and can detect objects even in conditions such as darkness, smoke, and fog. Thermal cameras are used in areas such as security, fire detection, and search and rescue.

Night Vision Cameras: Night vision cameras are specially designed to provide clear images even in low-light or dark environments. They provide night vision capability using technologies such as infrared illumination or thermal imaging.

Each technology has different advantages and may be preferred depending on the usage scenarios.

Radio Communication Technologies: The rapid development of electronics and semiconductor technologies in the last century has led to significant technical advances in communications. Telegraph, telephone, and internet communications, which started with wired transmission, have been replaced by wireless communication in some areas with the developing technological possibilities. Especially with the start of wireless and mobile phone calls, it has spread rapidly due to the significant advantages it provides to users, and the demand for quality parameters such as voice quality, bandwidth, and coverage area has increased.

Wireless communication technologies are systems that provide data communication, primarily voice, through wireless communication. These technologies are widely used by law enforcement, emergency teams, security units, and other professional groups.

Analog Radios: Traditional analog radios allow voice to be converted into electronic signals and transmitted wirelessly. Analog radios are a simple and economical communication solution, but they can have limited features. The frequencies used in analog radios can be licensed or unlicensed.

Digital Radios: Digital radios enable the transmission of voice and data by converting them into digital signals. Digital communication offers advantages such as higher voice quality, better background noise cancellation, and greater data transfer capacity. The protocols used in these radios are usually standardized, for example, digital mobile radio (DMR) or Project 25 (P25).

Trunking Systems: Trunking systems are complex systems in which radio communications are managed over a network. In these systems, users use channels from a shared pool instead of a specific frequency. Trunking systems make radio traffic more efficient by providing more effective frequency management, capacity optimization, and better incident management.

Remote Microphones and Speakers: Some radio systems can be integrated with remote microphones and speakers to provide users with hands-free communication. These devices remotely manage the microphone and speakers to provide voice communication while the user keeps the radio device attached to their body.

Emergency Buttons: Walkie-talkies are often equipped with emergency buttons. These buttons are used to quickly report an emergency or request support. When the emergency button is pressed, a predetermined emergency signal or alert is sent to other users.

Global Position Tracking Systems: Satellite positioning systems are mainly used in military fields (unmanned aircraft, smart bombs, positioning of all kinds of military vehicles and equipment, etc.) and scientific research (GIS applications, monitoring changes in geomorphological appearance, geological studies, remote sensing studies, geodetic measurements, cartography, etc.).

On the other hand, such systems are widely used in all transportation systems, mining activities, security applications, search and rescue operations, agricultural activities, and sportive activities. Global position tracking systems are technologies that can detect and track location through a worldwide satellite network. Global position tracking systems are used to determine and track the real-time location of objects or people.

Global Positioning System (GPS) Tracking Devices: Global positioning tracking devices can be portable or installed in vehicles. These devices receive GPS signals to determine the location of the device and transmit this location to a central server, enabling real-time tracking. GPS tracking devices can be used in many areas such as vehicle tracking, fleet management, security, and emergency management.

Transmission of Location Data: GPS tracking devices can transmit location data through a communication network at set intervals or in response to specific events. This is usually accomplished through a mobile data connection, GSM network, or satellite communications. The transmitted location data is stored on a central server and made accessible through monitoring platforms.

Real-time Tracking and Mapping: GPS tracking systems enable real-time mapping and display of location data on tracking platforms. These platforms display the location of the monitored assets (vehicles, equipment, people, etc.) on the map and allow tracking of their movements. In this way, you can monitor the instantaneous location of assets, plan their routes, and analyze their past movements.

Alerts and Notifications: GPS tracking systems can send automatic alerts and notifications when certain events or parameters are met. For example, you can receive instant alerts for traveling outside a designated zone or exceeding speed limits. This feature is important for safety, reliability, and efficiency.

Reporting and Analysis: GPS tracking systems enable reporting and analysis by recording historical location data. This data can include asset movement history, downtime, speed analysis, and other metrics. These reports can be used for performance evaluation, productivity analysis, and planning processes.

Databases and Information Systems: The software system used to define, create, use, and modify database systems and to meet any operational requirements related to database systems is called a "Database management system". Database management systems, also called DBMS for short, are very comprehensive system software. Databases and information systems are important components that provide effective storage, management, and access to information.

Database: A database is a system for storing structured and relational data. Databases organize information using data structures such as tables, columns, and rows. Databases are used to maintain data integrity, ensure data security, and provide fast access to data.

Database Management System (DBMS): A database management system is software that manages operations such as creating, updating, and accessing a database. A DBMS provides data access to database users, maintains data integrity, ensures database security, and optimizes database performance. Example DBMSs include MySQL, Oracle, Microsoft SQL Server, and PostgreSQL.

Relational Databases: Relational databases are a type of database in which data is structured using tables and relationships. In relational databases, data can be combined, queried, and analyzed using relationships between tables. Relational databases use constraints and references to ensure data consistency.

Information Systems: Information systems are structures that enable knowledge creation through the processing and analysis of data. Information systems consist of hardware, software, and processes to process, store, analyze data and report results. Examples include customer relationship management (CRM) systems, enterprise resource planning (ERP) systems, and decision support systems (DSS).

Database Security: Database security involves protecting data against unauthorized access, data loss, or data corruption. Database security includes various security measures such as user authorization, data encryption, and backup and restore methods.

Authentication Technologies: Authentication technologies are methods used to identify and verify the identity of a user or device. The most commonly used authentication method in authentication systems is to use a user number and password, as in other systems. User numbers and passwords can be kept in a private database or in a database shared by many systems.

In biometric systems, anatomical features such as face shape, fingerprints, palm prints, voice, and iris are used to identify a person, as well as behavioral features such as gait, mannerisms, gestures, and signature. Since these characteristics are unique to the individual, biometric systems are used in the development of biometric authentication. Biometric authentication is generally very secure and non-artificial in identifying users who want to log in to medical information systems. Biometric authentication is also an irrefutable authentication method. These technologies are used to increase security, prevent unauthorized access, and ensure access to the right person or device.

Password-based Authentication: Password-based authentication is a basic authentication method that uses information such as a username and password. The user gains access to the system when they provide the correct combination. For security, it is important to use strong passwords and password policies.

Two-Factor Authentication (2FA): Two-factor authentication uses two separate authentication factors to verify users' identities. These can typically take the form of knowing something (e.g., a password) and having something (e.g., a one-time code generated by a mobile phone or authentication app). This method increases security and prevents unauthorized access.

Biometric Authentication: Biometric authentication verifies a user's identity using physical or behavioral characteristics. Biometric characteristics such as fingerprints, facial recognition, voice recognition, retinal scanning, and finger veins can be used. This method provides high security because biometric characteristics are difficult to copy or forge.

Card or ID-based Verification: This method uses physical cards or identity documents such as ID cards, smart cards, or radio frequency identification (RFID) tags. The data stored on the card is read to verify the identity of the user. For example, credit cards, debit cards, or ID cards are examples of such authentication methods.

Third-Party Authentication: Third-party authentication involves a trusted third-party service provider managing the authentication process. These service providers verify the user's identity and provide access to another service or application. For example, social media platforms or login providers used in online services fall into this category.

Investigative and Investigative Technologies: Law enforcement agencies use a variety of technological and investigative tools to investigate crimes and identify criminals.

Crime Scene Investigation Equipment: Criminal investigation teams use cameras, measuring instruments, and other equipment at the crime scene. Officers use traditional investigative methods as well as technological devices to solve cases. These methods may include fingerprint collection, evidence collection, taking witness statements, and examining crime scenes.

Specialized Software: Computer-based software is used for crime analysis, evidence management, and incident tracking. Analyzing data from computers, cell phones, and other digital devices is important for cybercrime and collecting digital evidence. It also facilitates the investigation of criminals.

Chemical and Biological Laboratory Studies: These laboratories are used for DNA analysis, blood tests, drug tests, and other biological and chemical analyses.

Ballistics Laboratory Studies: Used to analyze the bullets and the weapons from which they are fired. These analyses help trace crime weapons and the bullets fired.

Alcohol and Drug Testing Kits: Law enforcement agencies use rapid test kits to detect alcohol and drugs.

Chemical Detection Devices: Used to detect hazardous chemical substances, these devices are important for identifying chemical attacks or areas where hazardous substances are present.

These research and investigation tools help law enforcement solve crimes and bring criminals to justice. These tools are constantly being improved to increase the effectiveness of criminal investigations.

REFERENCES

Baldwin, D. A. (1997). The concept of security. *Review of International Studies*, *23*(1), 5–26.

Berghel, H. (2017). The Internet of Things (IoT) and law enforcement: How technology impacts law enforcement practices. *Computer*, *50*(9), 87–91.

Bhattacherjee, A. (2012). *Social Science Research: Principles, Methods, and Practices (2nd ed.)*. Tampa, FL: University of South Florida. ISBN: 978-1475146127.

Bueermann, J. (2012). Being smarter about crime control: Law enforcement, science, and evidence-based practices. *NIJ Journal*, *269*, 14–19.

Chen, H., Chiang, R. H., & Storey, V. C. (2004). Business intelligence and analytics: From big data to big impact. *MIS Quarterly*, *36*(4), 1165–1188.

Cooper, R. G. (2014). New products: The critical success factors. *Marketing Management*, *14*(4), 12–13.

Creswell, J. W. (2014). *Research Design: Qualitative, Quantitative, and Mixed Methods Approaches (4th ed.)*. Thousand Oaks, CA: SAGE Publications. ISBN: 978-1452226101.

Drucker, P. F. (2002). *Innovation and Entrepreneurship: Practice and Principles*. New York: Harper Business. ISBN: 978-0060851132.

Gupta, K., & Gupta, A. (2018). *Information security and privacy in IoT: Models, Aalgorithms, and implementations*. Springer.

Jasanoff, S. (2006). Technology as a site and object of politics. *Science and Public Policy*, *33*(10), 707–716.

Jones, T., & Newburn, T. (2013). *Policing and technology: The impact of innovation on law enforcement practices*. Palgrave Macmillan.

Mankins, J. C. (2009). Technology readiness assessments: A retrospective. *Acta Astronautica, 65(9–10)*, 1216–1223.

Rogers, E. M. (2003). *Diffusion of innovations.* Free Press.

Sauser, B. J., Verma, D., Ramirez-Marquez, J. E., & Gove, R. (2006). From TRL to SRL: The concept of systems readiness levelsB Sauser, D Verma, J Ramirez-Marquez, R Gove - *Conference on Systems Engineering Research.* Los Angeles, CA.

Schneier, B. (2004). *Secrets and lies: Digital security in a networked world.* Wiley.

Schilling, M. A. (2017). *Strategic Management of Technological Innovation (5th ed.).* New York: McGraw-Hill Education. ISBN: 978-1259539060.

Stallings, W. (2015). *Computer organization and architecture: Designing for performance.* Pearson Education.

Tanenbaum, A. S., & Wetherall, D. J. (2011). *Computer networks.* Prentice Hall.

Tidd, J., & Bessant, J. (2018). *Managing Innovation: Integrating Technological, Market and Organizational Change (6th ed.).* Hoboken, NJ: Wiley. ISBN: 978-1119379454

Wheelwright, S. C., & Clark, K. B. (1992). *Revolutionizing Product Development: Quantum Leaps in Speed, Efficiency, and Quality.* New York: The Free Press. ISBN: 978-0029055151

Electronically based reconnaissance, surveillance, and detection systems

2.1 IMPORTANCE OF RECONNAISSANCE, SURVEILLANCE, AND DETECTION SYSTEMS

Reconnaissance, surveillance, and detection systems are technological systems used to identify and track targets, objects, or events in various fields. These systems can be equipped with different sensors and are often used in military, security, aerospace, space, reconnaissance, research, and civilian fields. A visualization of basic reconnaissance, surveillance, and detection systems is presented in Figure 2.1.

Unmanned Aerial Vehicles (UAVs) and Satellite Reconnaissance Systems: Unmanned aerial vehicles (drones) and satellite systems offer the ability to observe from high altitudes or remotely. While UAVs can provide high-quality imagery at low prices, satellites and airplanes require high altitude, cloud penetration, and other capabilities to take clear pictures. UAVs, on the other hand, fly at lower altitudes, allowing them to obtain clear images. Satellite reconnaissance systems can monitor and map large areas of the Earth's surface (Kim et al., 2019).

Electro-Optical and Infrared Cameras: Electro-optical cameras are used to detect objects and targets using the visible light spectrum, while infrared cameras produce thermal images by detecting infrared radiation emitted by objects.

Radio Frequency and Radar Systems: Radio frequency and radar systems can detect targets using electromagnetic waves. Radars are used for tracking and remote sensing of air, sea, and land platforms.

Acoustic and Sonar Systems: Acoustic and sonar systems use sound waves to detect underwater objects or submarines. Such systems play an important role in submarine detection and underwater exploration.

X-rays and Gamma Rays: Outside the medical field, X-rays and gamma rays can be used to view the internal structure of objects. Examples include baggage screening devices and security detection in areas such as airports.

Chemical Sensing and Biosensors: Chemical sensing systems are used for the detection of gases and chemical compounds in the atmosphere.

DOI: 10.1201/9781003597445-2

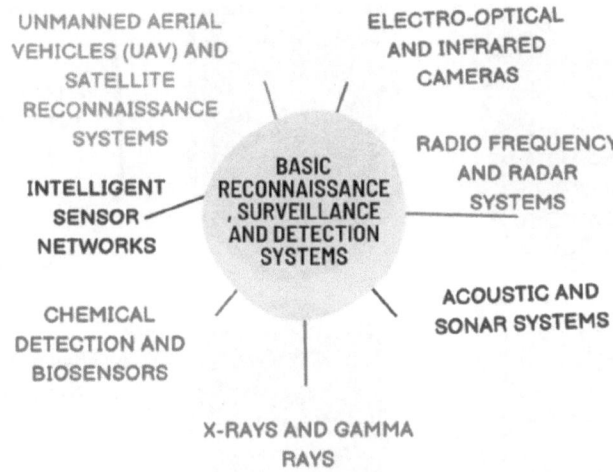

Figure 2.1 Basic reconnaissance, surveillance, and detection systems

Biosensors can be used to analyze biological samples and detect biological agents.

Smart Sensor Networks: Smart sensor networks are systems where multiple sensors work in coordination and data is collected in a centralized system. Such networks provide comprehensive monitoring and reconnaissance capabilities.

These systems are just some examples in the field of reconnaissance, surveillance, and detection. With technological advances, more advanced and integrated reconnaissance systems will continue to provide more effective and powerful detection capabilities in a variety of areas. Reconnaissance, surveillance, and detection systems are essential for law enforcement security because they play a critical role in combating a wide range of threats and crimes. The important topics of reconnaissance, surveillance, and detection systems for law enforcement are presented in Figure 2.2.

Early Detection and Prevention of Threats: Reconnaissance, surveillance, and detection systems help detect potential threats at an early stage. This allows law enforcement agencies to take quick and effective measures to prevent or minimize attacks.

Ensuring Public Safety: These systems play an important role in ensuring security in public spaces. To protect public safety, law enforcement agencies use reconnaissance and surveillance technologies to detect and respond to potential threats and criminal activities.

Effectiveness in Fighting Crime: Law enforcement agencies increase their ability to detect and apprehend criminals when equipped with such technological systems in the fight against crime. Cameras, sensors, and other surveillance systems help identify activity at crime scenes and collect evidence.

Figure 2.2 Important topics of reconnaissance, surveillance, and detection systems

Detection of Security Breaches: Reconnaissance and surveillance systems facilitate the detection of breaches of security systems and adverse events such as theft. Technologies such as motion detection, thermal cameras, and alarms continuously monitor security-critical areas.

Crisis and Disaster Preparedness: These systems provide law enforcement agencies with the ability to react quickly and effectively during natural disasters or crisis situations. For example, in disaster situations, reconnaissance and surveillance technologies can be important tools for rescue operations.

Border Security and Counter-Terrorism: In border security and counter-terrorism, reconnaissance and surveillance systems help detect illegal crossings and terrorist activities. These systems are used to monitor and interdict threats at and across borders.

In general, reconnaissance, surveillance, and detection systems are important for law enforcement agencies because they help to provide rapid and effective responses in safety-critical areas. The use of such technological tools for crime fighting, public safety, and national security increases the effectiveness of law enforcement and plays an important role in ensuring the safety of society.

2.2 URBAN SECURITY MANAGEMENT SYSTEMS

Especially in the last decade, security has become a more important issue in cities around the world. The concept of security is recognized as not only protection from the outside with walls, but also as a factor affecting how cities are shaped. The relationship between security and urbanization is examined in terms of development and migration. Since security threats are considered to affect daily life and population movements, equipping cities with surveillance technologies seems to have become a part of every-day life. There are those who see this situation as positive, but there are also those who believe that it threatens privacy and certain anonymous freedoms (Fawaz, Harb, & Gharbieh, 2012). Urban security management systems refer to an integrated and centralized system designed to enhance the security of cities and respond to incidents quickly and effectively using modern technologies. These systems collect, analyze, and manage city-wide security-related data using different sensors, cameras, and software. In our country, the term MOBESE is gaining recognition among the public and in communication, while the concept of KGYS is gaining recognition in the public sector. Meanwhile, in international literature, the issue is addressed through the concept of KDTS (CCTV) (Kün, Bayram & Özhan, 2014). The main objectives of urban security management systems are to increase effi-ciency in security services, to detect security threats before they occur, to produce evidence that may be needed in forensic investigations, and to help ensure general public order and peace.

Urban security and management is a complex task that requires the effi-cient processing of many inputs. In order to manage this complex function effectively, in addition to the sensors that detect the city, data from institu-tions that perform different functions in city management are also needed (Türk & Komesli, 2013). The features and capabilities of urban security management systems are presented in Figure 2.3.

Surveillance and Monitoring: Urban security management systems con-tinuously monitor different areas of the city through cameras and other sen-sors, collecting real-time images and data. In this way, incidents and threats are quickly detected and responded to.

Motion Detection and Facial Recognition: The systems detect suspicious people and events using motion detection technology and facial recognition

URBAN SECURITY MANAGEMENT SYSTEMS

Surveillance and Monitoring	Motion Detection and Facial Recognition	Intelligent Video Analytics
Emergency and Alarm Management	Data Integration	Social Media and Digital Monitoring
GIS Integration	Data Analysis and Reporting	Night Vision and Thermal Monitoring

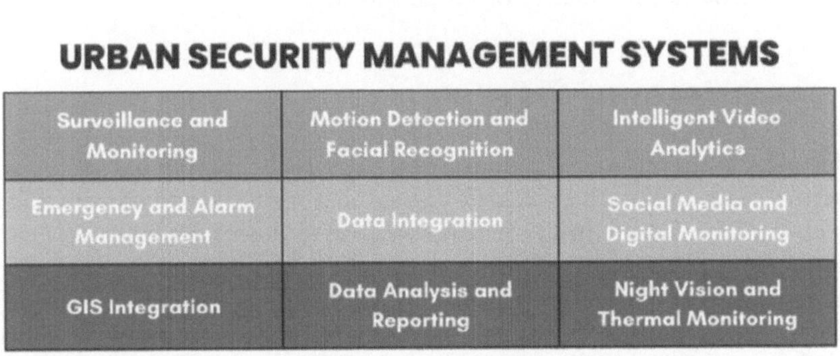

Figure 2.3 Features and capabilities of urban security management systems

software. Especially in crime scenes and critical areas, facial recognition technology is used to identify unauthorized individuals.

Intelligent Video Analytics: Urban security management systems automatically analyze images using intelligent video analytics. In this way, situations such as traffic density, parking violations, and abandoned luggage can be detected quickly.

Emergency and Alarm Management: Systems automatically generate alarms and notifications in emergency situations. In cases such as fires, terrorist attacks, and natural disasters, they transfer information to authorities and law enforcement agencies instantly, speeding up response processes.

Data Integration: Urban security management systems integrate data from different security systems and other organizations. It increases coordination by providing data sharing between law enforcement, fire brigades, health services, and other emergency units.

Social Media and Digital Monitoring: The systems monitor posts made on social media and other digital platforms to detect dangerous situations. They provide information to security forces, especially during social events and protests.

GIS Integration: Urban security management systems integrate with geographic information systems (GIS) to show the location and distribution of incidents on a map. In this way, response plans can be created more efficiently.

Data Analysis and Reporting: The systems analyze the collected data to generate crime analysis, trends, and statistics. With these analyses, city security strategies and policies can be developed.

Night Vision and Thermal Monitoring: Urban security management systems provide effective monitoring in low light conditions and at night with night vision technologies and thermal cameras.

Urban security management systems provide more robust and integrated monitoring and response capabilities to security forces and city governments. These systems play an important role in maintaining social peace, combating crime, providing rapid response to emergencies, managing traffic, and improving the quality of life in the city.

2.3 BASIC IMAGING SYSTEMS

Under-vehicle surveillance systems are traditionally carried out by security personnel walking around a vehicle with a mirror on the end of a stick. This person can see underneath a mirrored vehicle to detect contraband such as weapons, bombs, or other security threats. The challenge arises, however, in that the mirror-on-a-stick approach allows only partial coverage underneath the vehicle, and the mirror is often restricted by ambient lighting conditions such as poor illumination or glare from sunlight (Koschan et al., 2004). Technological systems for observing and inspecting the underside

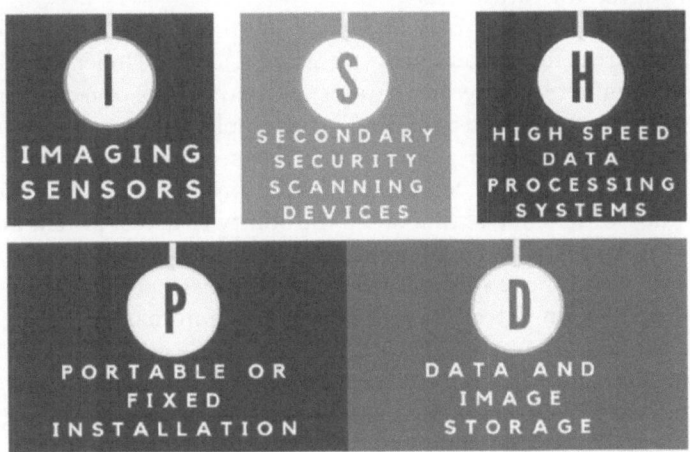

Figure 2.4 Main components of under-vehicle imaging systems

of vehicles have been developed. These systems are widely used in areas such as security, border control, counter-terrorism, and drug trafficking. Under-vehicle imaging systems help detect objects or hazardous materials hidden under vehicles and are commonly used at security checkpoints, ports, airports, and border crossings. Systems that create multi-perspective mosaics of infrared and color video data are being developed for under-vehicle inspection. The main components of under-vehicle imaging systems are presented in Figure 2.4.

Imaging Sensors: Special cameras and sensors used to observe the underside of the vehicle. Detailed images of the underside of the vehicle are usually obtained using high-resolution and wide-angle cameras.

Secondary Security Scanning Devices: While some under-vehicle imaging systems visually scan the underside of the vehicle, they can also be integrated with other security screening devices. For example, radiation detectors can also be used to detect radioactive materials during under-vehicle scans.

High-Speed Data Processing Systems: Under-vehicle imaging systems incorporate high-speed data processing algorithms and software to quickly process large amounts of data. In this way, they can quickly analyze possible threats under the vehicle.

Portable or Fixed Installation: Under-vehicle imaging systems can have either portable or fixed installations. Portable systems can be used in different locations to scan vehicles, while fixed installations are used permanently at specific security checkpoints.

Data and Image Storage: The systems have data and image storage infrastructure to store and archive scan results. In this way, past scan data and images are saved for future use.

Narrow, hard-to-reach areas and poor lighting make the underside of vehicles ideal areas for concealment (Ramadoss, 2003). Under-vehicle imaging systems can detect potential threats and dangerous objects even when they are hidden underneath vehicles. For example, they can detect dangerous objects such as explosives, weapons, drugs, or other illicit substances associated with smuggling. Such technologies provide security forces, port officials, and border control units with the ability to detect potential threats and illegal activities, effectively preventing and responding to them.

Photo trap systems are special camera systems designed to detect moving objects using motion detection technology and automatically take photos or videos. Photo trap systems generally have a single camera, work by activating the camera with a PIR sensor that detects motion at a certain distance, are used for automatic image and video recording, and have a wide range of uses. Photo trap systems available on the market scan a specific area depending on the angle of view of the camera used. Existing systems include a camera, motion sensor, storage unit, and microprocessor that enables the entire system to operate. In addition to these, there are optional add-ons such as Wi-Fi modules, SMS modules, e-mail services modules.

There are different types of photo trap systems used in areas such as defense, medical, environmental research, wildlife surveillance, reconnaissance and surveillance, scientific research, nest ecology, rare species detection, environmental population estimation and rich species identification, border security, illegal crossing detection, habitat invasion, orienteering, sports activities, military and civilian targets, and sports competitions (Virta, 2013). Law enforcement agencies also actively use photo trap systems in various fields for security and surveillance purposes. Examples of the use of photo trap systems by law enforcement agencies are presented in Figure 2.5.

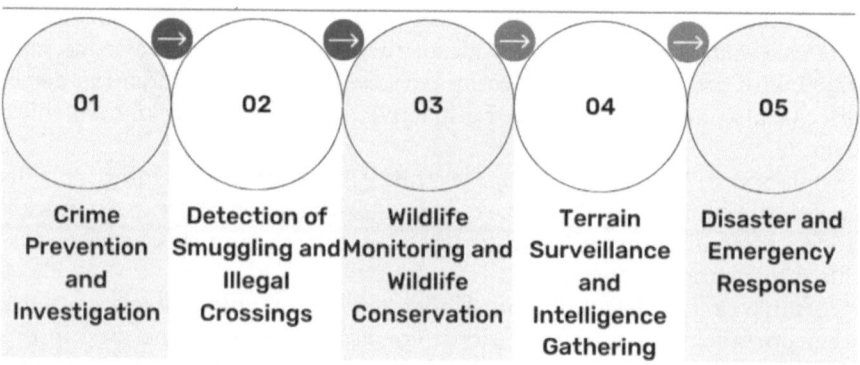

Figure 2.5 Examples of use of photo trap systems by law enforcement agencies

Crime Prevention and Investigation: Photo trap systems play an active role in crime prevention and investigation by being used at crime scenes or in areas where criminals may be operating. Thanks to motion detection sensors, when movement is detected in a certain area, the system automatically takes photos or videos, enabling the detection of possible crimes and the identification of criminals.

Detection of Smuggling and Illegal Crossings: Smuggling activities, border violations, and illegal crossings can be detected using photo trap systems at border checkpoints and critical areas. When these systems detect movement in a certain area, they record events and suspicious activities and alert security forces.

Wildlife Monitoring and Wildlife Conservation: Photo trap systems are used in wildlife sanctuaries and natural parks to monitor and protect rare and threatened species. Estimating population abundance is a theoretical and practical problem in wildlife management and conservation. It is important to protect animals by observing them in their natural habitat without disturbing them with human activities. Photo traps are used in this area to provide estimates of presence and population density through a camera that is activated when it receives information about the passage of a possible species (Luna, Alonso, & Ponce, 2019). These systems are effectively used to observe the behavior of native animals and track endangered species.

Terrain Surveillance and Intelligence Gathering: Photo trap systems can be used for land surveillance and intelligence gathering in border areas, military bases, or other areas of security importance. Through motion detection, dangerous persons or hostile elements can be detected approaching the area.

Disaster and Emergency Response: Photo trap systems are used in disaster areas and emergency response to help quickly assess incidents. Especially during natural disasters or search and rescue operations, photo traps are important tools to identify missing persons or dangerous situations.

Photo trap systems are an important technology that provides law enforcement with the ability to automatically detect and track incidents. Their motion detection and automatic photo or video capture capabilities help security forces respond quickly and effectively to incidents and prevent crimes. They are also of great importance in nature-oriented missions such as wildlife conservation and wildlife monitoring.

2.4 HIGH RESOLUTION SYSTEMS

Unmanned aerial vehicles (UAVs) and satellite surveillance systems are used as important tools for law enforcement security operations and incident tracking. Unmanned aerial vehicles (UAVs), also commonly known as drones or remotely piloted aircraft, have found wide application in the last few decades due to their high mobility and low cost. Historically, UAVs have primarily been used in the military domain, often deployed over the territory of hostile forces to reduce pilot casualties (Zeng, Zhang, & Lim, 2016). The uses of UAVs and satellite tracking systems by law enforcement agencies are presented in Figure 2.6.

Unmanned Aerial Vehicles (UAV) Monitoring Systems: UAVs are air vehicles controlled by remote control or automated systems. UAVs can be broadly divided into two categories: fixed-wing and rotary-wing, each with its own strengths and weaknesses. For example, fixed-wing UAVs are generally capable of high speed and heavy payloads, but they need to maintain constant forward motion to stay aloft and are therefore not suitable for stationary applications such as close inspection. In contrast, rotary-wing UAVs such as quadcopters have limited mobility and payload capacity, but can move in any direction and remain stationary in the air. They can be used on air, land, or sea platforms. Law enforcement agencies use UAVs to monitor and track crime scenes, illegal activities, and security threats. UAVs fly at low altitudes, providing real-time imagery and data so that law enforcement can have immediate information and respond quickly. Used in crime prevention and investigation, counter-terrorism, border security,

Figure 2.6 Areas of use of UAV and satellite tracking systems by law enforcement agencies

disaster response, and search and rescue operations, UAVs provide a critical advantage to security forces.

Satellite Tracking Systems: Satellite tracking systems are used to observe the earth's surface through orbiting satellite systems. Satellite systems can collect high-resolution imagery and data from the ground. Law enforcement agencies can use satellite tracking systems to track land, air, and maritime operations; ensure border security; assess disaster areas; and observe remote areas. Satellite surveillance systems provide strategic intelligence and situational awareness by covering large areas. In this way, law enforcement agencies can better analyze the security situation and make more informed decisions.

UAV and satellite surveillance systems provide law enforcement agencies with significant advantages in both security and operational capabilities. Fast and effective monitoring, early detection of security threats, strategic intelligence gathering, and remote area surveillance help law enforcement agencies manage incidents more effectively and ensure public safety. At the same time, these technologies give security forces greater flexibility and agility to better understand risks and respond efficiently.

Integrated Operational Use: UAV and satellite surveillance systems provide more effective operational utilization when used in an integrated manner by law enforcement agencies. UAVs can collect more detailed images and data at low altitudes that satellites cannot observe. In this way, security forces can better assess the situation on the ground and intervene quickly.

Special Missions and Covert Operations: UAVs and satellite tracking systems can be designed for use in special missions and covert operations. In covert operations, UAVs can perform important tasks such as intelligence gathering and target tracking, helping security forces provide intelligence without risk.

Disaster Response and Rescue Operations: UAV and satellite tracking systems can also be used effectively in rescue operations during natural disasters and emergencies. Satellite tracking systems can monitor disaster areas to help determine the extent of damage and direct rescue teams. UAVs can also be used in search and rescue operations in hazardous areas, providing an important tool for locating missing persons.

Data Analysis and Intelligence: UAVs and satellite surveillance systems are also used to analyze the data they collect and gather intelligence. This data is an important source for making strategic decisions in crime analysis, counter-terrorism, border security, and other security operations.

UAV and satellite surveillance systems provide law enforcement agencies with many security and intelligence advantages. These technologies enable security forces to be better informed, manage incidents faster and more effectively, and enhance public safety. Especially in crisis and emergency situations, the use of these systems facilitates rescue operations and plays a critical role in terms of security. With integrated use, UAV and satellite surveillance systems contribute to the security of society by increasing the security strength and effectiveness of law enforcement agencies.

2.5 NIGHT VISION SYSTEMS AND THERMAL CAMERAS

Behind-the-wall imaging systems are technological systems that play an important role in law enforcement security operations and search and rescue activities. These systems have the capability to identify and detect the position of objects or people behind walls. Examples of the use of behind-the-wall imaging systems by law enforcement agencies are presented in Figure 2.7.

Investigations: During criminal investigations, law enforcement agencies can use behind-the-wall imaging systems to look inside buildings where criminals or illegal activities are taking place. Thanks to RADAR technology, they can more effectively direct their operations by detecting objects or people hidden behind walls.

Hostage Rescue and Counter-Terrorism: In counter-terrorism and hostage rescue operations, behind-the-wall imaging systems help security forces analyze the situation inside the building. This allows security forces to pinpoint the location of hostage takers or terrorists and plan response strategies.

Disaster Rescue and Search Operations: In disasters or accidents, behind-the-wall imaging systems can be used to locate missing persons. These systems play an important role in detecting people trapped under rubble and directing rescue operations.

Border Security and Surveillance: Behind-the-wall imaging systems are also used in border security and surveillance. In border areas, they help detect illegal crossings or dangerous elements hidden behind walls.

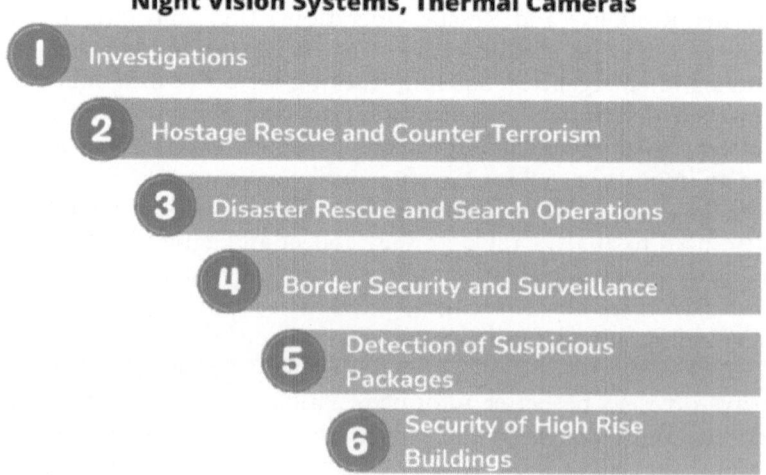

Figure 2.7 Use cases of behind-the-wall imaging systems

Detection of Suspicious Packages: Behind-the-wall imaging systems are used to detect threats such as suspicious packages or explosives. In this way, potential threats are quickly detected and measures are taken.

Security of High-Rise Buildings: Behind-the-wall surveillance systems can be used to enhance the security of high-rise buildings. They provide real-time information to security forces by monitoring movements inside the building.

Behind-the-wall imaging systems give law enforcement agencies a great advantage in detecting threats indoors or behind walls. Thanks to RADAR technology, security forces can conduct operations more effectively and safely by identifying hidden objects, people, or dangerous elements. It also plays a vital role in search and rescue operations and in the identification of missing persons.

Night vision systems are technological systems that help law enforcement officers work in security operations and in environments with limited visibility at night. These systems help to clearly see surrounding objects and people in low light conditions or in complete darkness. Night vision systems based on thermal imaging technology work by detecting infrared emissions (Rash, Verona & Crowley, 1990). Law enforcement agencies actively use night vision systems in various fields. Examples of the use of night vision systems by law enforcement agencies are presented in Figure 2.8 (Tsuji, et al., 2002).

Crime Prevention and Investigation: Night vision systems give security forces an advantage in crime scenes and dangerous areas. At night, the frequency of crimes may increase and visibility may decrease. Night vision technology enables security forces to more effectively patrol and conduct crime prevention operations at night.

Border Security: At border checkpoints and critical border areas, night vision systems are used to detect illegal crossings and enhance border security. These systems help monitor border activity and potential threats at night.

Search and Rescue Operations: Night vision systems are used to detect missing or endangered persons and guide rescue operations. Night vision technology is a vital tool, especially when search and rescue teams work in dark and challenging conditions.

Crime Prevention and Investigation

Border Security

Search and Rescue Operations

Counter Terrorism and Special Operations

Wildlife Protection

Figure 2.8 Examples of use of night vision systems by law enforcement agencies

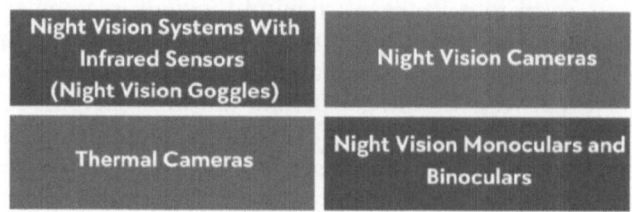

Figure 2.9 Examples of use of night vision systems by law enforcement agencies

Counter-Terrorism and Special Operations: Night vision systems are used in counter-terrorism and special operations, helping security forces track targets and operate in dangerous areas. Such operations are often carried out at night, and night vision technology increases the advantage of security forces.

Wildlife Protection: Night vision systems are also used in wildlife conservation and wildlife monitoring projects. By using them in wildlife areas at night to observe rare or threatened species, researchers and conservation teams can monitor the behavior of native animals.

Night vision systems give law enforcement agencies the ability to operate more effectively and efficiently at night. When visibility is low and low light conditions are challenging, night vision technology gives law enforcement an advantage and enables them to respond quickly to incidents. Under challenging conditions, such as low illumination, adverse weather conditions, and the presence of obstructive objects, unassisted sighted cross-country flight by aviators using existing field systems, although possible, can be extremely dangerous (Rash, Verona & Crowley, 1990). These systems play an important role in enhancing the safety of society by being used as a critical tool in safety and rescue operations. The basic technologies of night vision systems are presented in Figure 2.9.

Night Vision Systems with Infrared Sensors (Night Vision Goggles): Night vision systems with infrared sensors contain sensors that are sensitive to thermal infrared rays emitted by objects and people. Such systems detect the heat emitted by objects and organisms and convert it into images. Based on temperature differences in the environment, these systems effectively provide images even in low light conditions or complete darkness.

Night Vision Cameras: Night vision cameras are specially designed to operate in low light conditions. These cameras can detect and image objects even when the surrounding light level is low. Some night vision cameras can work in conjunction with special IR illumination to further improve image quality.

Thermal Cameras: Thermal cameras create images by detecting infrared radiation emitted by objects. Thermal cameras are passive sensors that capture infrared radiation emitted by objects above absolute zero. Originally designed for military surveillance and night vision, in recent years they have become more accessible for a wider range of uses. The use of such sensors in imaging systems plays an important role in overcoming the illumination challenges of traditional grayscale or RGB cameras (Gade & Moeslund, 2014).

Thermal cameras are a commonly used technology in night vision systems and work particularly effectively in low light conditions.

Night Vision Monoculars and Binoculars: Night vision monoculars and binoculars are portable night vision systems. These devices use night vision technology to give users a better view in low light conditions. Night vision binoculars are used for a variety of purposes, ranging from military operations to nighttime use by tourists in nature.

Night vision systems provide effective images in low light conditions with different technologies, enabling security forces to manage night operations more effectively. These systems play an important role in various fields such as crime prevention and investigation, border security, search and rescue operations, counter-terrorism, and protection of natural life at night. Thanks to their high technology and advanced detection capabilities, night vision systems give security forces the upper hand in critical operations and are used as an important tool to enhance public safety.

REFERENCES

Fawaz, M., Harb, M., & Gharbieh, A. (2012). Living Beirut's security zones: An investigation of the modalities and practice of urban security. *City & Society*, 24(2), 173–195

Gade, R., & Moeslund, T. B. (2014). Thermal cameras and applications: A survey. Machine vision and applications, 25, 245–262.

Kim, J., Kim, S., Ju, C., & Son, H. I. (2019). Unmanned aerial vehicles in agriculture: A review of perspective of platform, control, and applications. *Ieee Access*, 7, 105100–105115.

Koschan, A., Page, D., Ng, J. C., Abidi, M., Gorsich, D., & Gerhart, G. (2004). SAFER under vehicle inspection through video mosaic building. *Industrial Robot: An International Journal*, 31(5), 435–442.

Kün, U., Bayram, L., & Özhan, M. Z. (2014). Urban Security Management Systems. Basic Strategies in Security Sector, Chapter 12, Nobel Publications.

Luna, L. S., Alonso, J. M. M., & Ponce, L. A. E. (2019). Desarrollo Del Sistema Integral Foto-Trampa Para La Detección De Fauna (Development Of The Integral Photo-Trap System For Wildlife Detection). *Pistas Educativas*, 41(133), 625–642.

Ramadoss, B. (2003). *Hardware and software development of a wireless imaging system for under vehicle inspection robot.* Project In-Lieu Of Thesis (PILOT) Report, University of Tennessee, Knoxville, TN, USA.

Rash, C. E., Verona, R. W., & Crowley, J. S. (1990). Human factors and safety considerations of night-vision systems flight using thermal imaging systems. In *Helmet-mounted displays II* (Vol. 1290, pp. 142–164). SPIE.

Türk, M., & Komesli, M. (2013). Semantic network based information sharing for Urban security management systems components. *International Journal of Scientific and Technological Research,* 2(1), 1–7.

Tsuji, T., Hattori, H., Watanabe, M., & Nagaoka, N. (2002). Development of night-vision system. *IEEE Transactions on Intelligent Transportation Systems,* 3(3), 203–209.

Virta, S. (2013). Governing urban security in Finland: Towards the 'European model'. *European Journal of Criminology,* 10(3), 341–353.

Zeng, Y., Zhang, R., & Lim, T. J. (2016). Wireless communications with unmanned aerial vehicles: Opportunities and challenges. *IEEE Communications Magazine,* 54(5), 36–42.

Chapter 3

Electronically based controlled access systems to buildings and facilities

3.1 INTRODUCTION

The technologies used for the physical protection of buildings and facility areas constitute controlled access systems. These technologies are presented in Figure 3.1.

Camera Systems: They consist of cameras, hardware, and monitoring systems used to monitor a specific area and create time-based video recordings. It is very important to automatically process the images of surveillance cameras at border posts, cameras regulating traffic flow, and security cameras protecting individual areas.

Without image processing, a security camera can only record events. With image processing, threats and suspicious activities can be detected and prevented in advance. These systems are usually integrated with surveillance and other detection systems (Erkan, Özçalık, & Yılmaz, 2015). The camera system visualization is presented in Figure 3.2.

Motion Detection Sensors: They consist of sensors and electronics used to detect movement. Motion detectors are available as part of a burglar alarm that can alert the homeowner or security service when it detects the movement of a potential intruder. They can also activate the security camera by detecting possible intrusion.

Alarm Systems: Criminals often attack structures that are much more vulnerable than those protected by security alarm systems. These systems warn of unauthorized entry or danger. They can work through methods such as audible alarms, sirens, or warning messages. Some of today's modern security alarm systems include home burglar alarms, threat alarms, industrial alarms, and speed alarms (Ahmad et al., 2019).

Access Control Systems: Systems used to control access to a specific area. They can use authentication methods such as cards, keys, fingerprints, or facial recognition.

Biometric Security Technologies: The automatic identification/verification of an individual's identity based on the analysis of their biological (biometric) characteristics is generally known as biometrics technology (Alsaadi, 2015). It provides authentication and access control using physical

DOI: 10.1201/9781003597445-3

Figure 3.1 Technologies used for physical protection of buildings and facilities

or behavioral characteristics of individuals. Technologies such as finger-print readers, facial recognition systems, retinal scanning systems, and voice recognition systems fall into this category.

These classifications provide an overview of security technologies, but more specialized and advanced technologies can also be found within each category.

3.2 IMPORTANCE OF BUILDING AND FACILITY SECURITY

Law enforcement agencies can consider the importance of securing build-ings and facilities from a variety of perspectives. These topics are presented in Figure 3.3.

Public Safety: Secure buildings and facilities reduce potential threats to the public and lower the risk of crime, thus ensuring the safety of the community.

Preventive Measures: Law enforcement officers take measures to prevent potential crimes and increase security by ensuring the safety of buildings and facilities.

Figure 3.2 Camera visualization

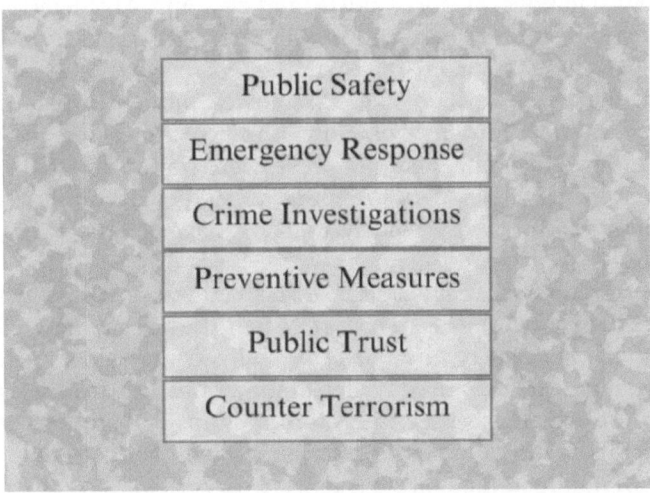

Figure 3.3 Headings on the importance of ensuring building and facility security

Emergency Response: Disaster, in the most general terms, is an event that occurs when people do not expect it and causes various damages. By providing a rapid response in critical situations, it minimizes the loss of life and property and creates a resilient society against disasters. Advances in technology offer new opportunities and have the potential to change existing technologies. While applications such as satellite systems, fax machines, television, and short message service were effective in disaster management in the past, innovations such as the Internet of Things, artificial intelligence, robots, and smart systems have greater importance today (Memiş & Babaoğlu, 2020).

Public Trust: The public trusts the security of buildings and facilities. This improves the quality of life and stimulates economic activity.

Crime Investigations: Security measures make it easier and more effective to conduct investigations in buildings and facilities where crimes have been committed.

Counter-Terrorism: Security of buildings and facilities plays an important role in preventing and mitigating terrorist attacks.

For these reasons, law enforcement agencies continuously strive to ensure building and facility security and play an important role in the welfare and safety of society.

3.3 TOP SEARCH SYSTEMS

Body search systems are devices generally used for security purposes and are designed to detect potential threats by being used at entrances and exits of buildings, facilities, airports, ports, and customs. The detection areas of body search systems are presented in Figure 3.4.

X-ray Scanning Systems: X-ray scanning systems use X-rays to image the internal structure of objects. These systems scan metals, plastics, liquids, and other materials to detect potential threats. Improving the process of X-ray scanning of passenger bags to prevent prohibited objects from passing through the security checkpoint remains a key focus (Von Bastian, Michel & Schwaninger, 2011). It is widely used for baggage and cargo screening at airports.

Metal Detectors: Metal detectors use magnetic fields to detect metal objects on people or objects. They are often used at security checkpoints to prevent the concealed carry of guns, knives, and other metal objects. One of the oldest devices used to detect metal objects was the electromagnetic detector, which was used to locate handguns and other metallic items. However, this technique was not sensitive enough to prevent hijackings where small non-metallic objects (such as box cutters) were used as knives, as in events such as 9/11. These detectors are not effective in detecting small non-metallic weapons or knives (Zentai, 2010).

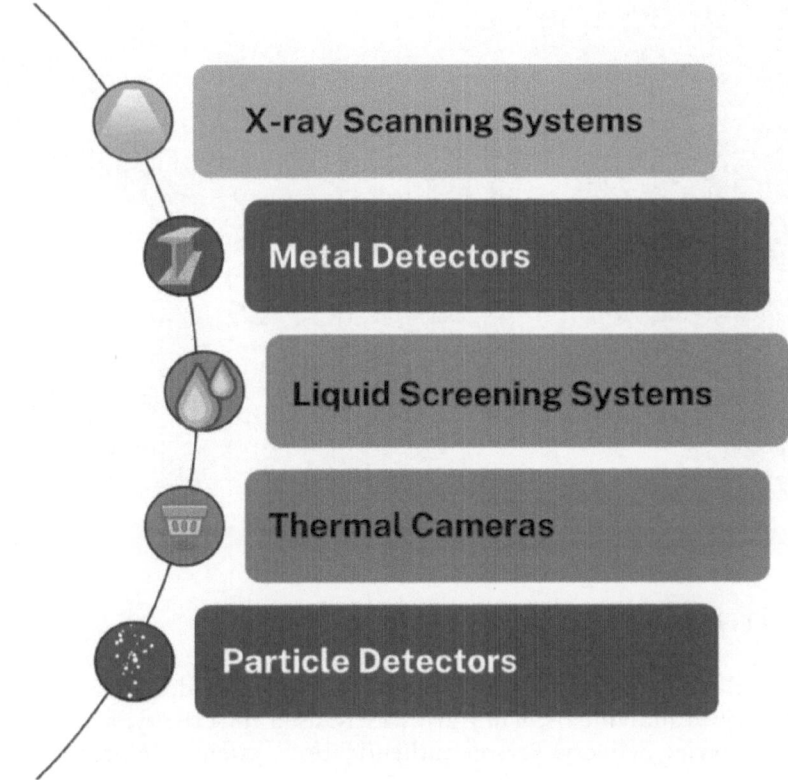

Figure 3.4 Detection areas of top search systems

Liquid Screening Systems: These systems screen liquids by chemical analysis and identify hazardous liquids. They are used to control the transportation of liquids at airports, customs, and special security areas.

Thermal Cameras: Thermal cameras use infrared light to detect and display the surface temperature of objects. These systems are used to detect objects at night or in low light conditions. There are thermal cameras used for security purposes, search and rescue operations, and fire detection. An image taken with a thermal camera is presented in Figure 3.5.

Particle Detectors: Particle detectors are used to detect radiation and nuclear materials. They are used at nuclear facilities, customs, and border crossings to prevent the escape of nuclear materials.

These pat-down systems can be used by security personnel to help detect potential threats and ensure security. However, their use should be supervised, taking into account privacy and ethical considerations.

Figure 3.5 Image taken with thermal camera

3.4 AUTHENTICATION SYSTEMS

Person authentication systems are technologies used to identify and verify the identity of individuals. They are widely used in security, access control, and service delivery. Person authentication systems are presented in Figure 3.6.

Biometric Authentication: Biometric authentication is a method of verifying the identity of individuals using their physiological or behavioral characteristics. Biometric data such as fingerprints, retinal scans, facial recognition, voice analysis, and finger vein scans uniquely identify individuals and are used as a reliable method of authentication.

Biometrics-based authentication systems usually involve the same processes. They consist of two main phases: The enrollment process and the exit process. In the enrollment phase, the user's biometric data is collected, analyzed, and used to create a unique template, which is then stored in a database. In the exit phase, the person's data is compared with the templates in the database and authentication is performed. This process is used in many biometric authentication techniques (Alsaadi, 2015).

Card-based Authentication: In this method, individuals are authenticated using specially designed cards. ID cards usually contain personal information, a picture, and, in some cases, biometric data. These cards are used for access control, bank transactions, and authentication in public services.

Passwords and PIN Codes: One of the most common methods for individual authentication is to use a username and password or PIN code.

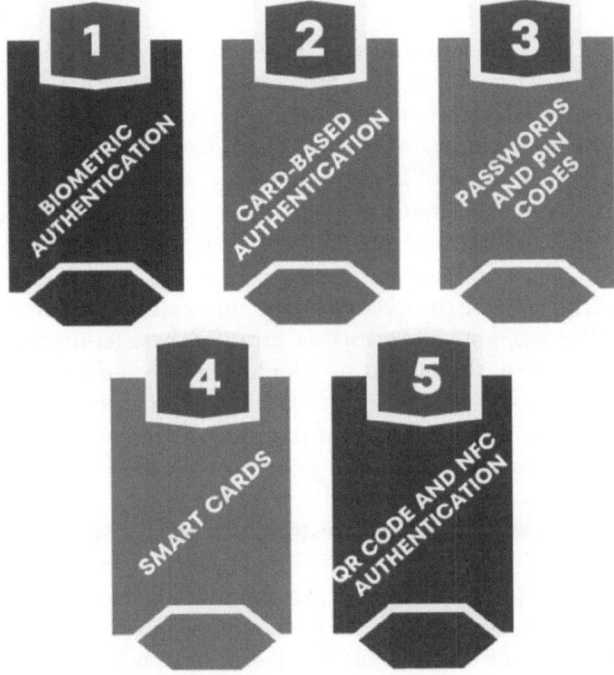

Figure 3.6 Individual authentication systems

Authentication is performed by entering a combination of a username and password or just a PIN code. However, these methods can be weak in terms of security, so stronger authentication methods should be preferred.

Smart Cards: Smart cards are cards that contain microprocessors and memory and enable authentication by storing personal information. With personal data and security keys, these cards can be used for physical access, digital signatures, and online authentication. These smart chip cards contain a chip that usually has several megabytes of RAM. They can also be used to perform cryptographic operations such as RSA public key cryptography, signature creation, and verification through special circuits (Shelfer & Procaccino, 2002).

QR Code and NFC Authentication: QR codes and NFC (Near Field Communication) tags can be used with smartphones and other devices to facilitate authentication. The QR code or NFC tag on the ID document or card is read through authentication apps to confirm identity.

These personal authentication systems have an important role to play in enhancing security and preventing crimes such as identity theft. However, choosing the right and reliable authentication methods is critical to ensuring security.

3.5 ALARM SYSTEMS

Alarm systems used for building and facility security are technological systems that help increase security by detecting various threats. These systems are designed to identify potential dangers such as burglary, fire, and gas leakage and to give a quick warning. Here are some examples of alarm systems used in building and facility security:

Theft Alarm Systems: Intrusion alarm systems are systems that are triggered in the event of unauthorized entry or theft into buildings or facilities. Using devices such as door sensors, window sensors, and motion detectors, the alarm is triggered in the event of any abnormality within the defined secure zone. Burglar alarm security is initiated by a comprehensive loop of automatic circuitry, the output of which is connected to an alarm or an indicator that informs the owner of the danger. These systems typically include a centralized control box that monitors different motion indicators and perimeter sensors that alert and notify the owner or authorities when any of these sensors are triggered (Silvano et al., 2012).

Fire Alarm Systems: Fire alarm systems are used to detect fire hazards in buildings or facilities. Various sensors are used as sensors in fire alarm systems. Smoke sensor, flame sensor, temperature sensor, and light sensor are the main sensors used, and the most commonly used sensor is the smoke sensor. A smoke sensor can be considered a light sensor. The smoke sensor module consists of a linear beam emitting light source and a photodiode. Smoke entering the sensor module blocks the light transmission from the light source to the photodiode and causes a fire alarm. In fire alarm systems using temperature sensors, the system gives an alarm when the temperature rises above a certain value. There are also fire detection systems that use smoke sensors and temperature sensors at the same time. These systems are sensitive to both temperature and smoke and are more effective in fire detection (Çeltek et al., 2017). These systems minimize the loss of life and property by providing early fire warnings.

Gas Leak Alarm Systems: Gas leak alarm systems are systems that sound alarms in the event of leaks of natural gas or other hazardous gases. Gas sensors detect dangerous gas levels in the air and alert users when the alarm is triggered. These systems are effective in reducing the risk of explosion or poisoning from gas leaks.

Emergency Alarm Systems: Emergency alarm systems are used in emergency situations in buildings or facilities. These systems provide fast and effective warnings in different scenarios such as fire, theft, and medical emergencies. Emergency buttons or panels can be part of such systems.

CCTV and Detection Systems: Closed Circuit Television (CCTV) cameras and detection systems are used to monitor the perimeter of buildings and facilities and detect anomalies. Thanks to motion detection sensors and video analysis technology, alarms can be triggered, and security personnel can receive instant alerts.

These alarm systems play an important role in enhancing building and facility security. Rapid alarming when abnormal conditions are detected enables early detection of hazards and quick response. Thanks to advanced technologies and integration options, alarm systems for building and facility security have become more effective and versatile.

REFERENCES

Ahmad, M. B., Muhammad, A. S., Abdullahi, A. A., Tijjani, A., Iliyasu, A. S., Muhammad, I. M., ... & Sani, K. M. (2019). Need for security alarm system installation and their challenges faced. *International Journal of New Computer Architectures and Their Applications*, 9(3), 68–76.

Alsaadi, I. M. (2015). Physiological biometric authentication systems, advantages, disadvantages and future development: A review. *International Journal of Scientific & Technology Research*, 4(12), 285–289.

Çeltek, S. A., Durgun, M., Gökrem, L., & Durgun, Y. (2017). Design and implementation of internet of things based fire alarm system. *Gaziosmanpaşa Scientific Research Journal*, 6(3), 66–72.

Erkan, E., Özçalık, H. R., & Yılmaz, Ş. (2015). Designing a smart security camera system. In *2015 23rd signal processing and communications applications Conference* (SIU) (pp. 1705–1708). IEEE.

Memiş, L., & Babaoğlu, C. (2020). Process approach and technology in emergency and disaster management. *Journal of Ömer Halisdemir University Faculty of Economics and Administrative Sciences*, 13(4), 1–12.

Shelfer, K. M., & Procaccino, J. D. (2002). Smart card evolution. *Communications of the ACM*, 45(7), 83–88.

Silvano, B., Oscar, R., Claudio, L., & Marco, A. (2012). A Wireless Sensor Network ad-hoc designed as anti-theft alarm system for photovoltaic panels. *Wireless Sensor Network*.

Von Bastian, C. C., Michel, S., & Schwaninger, A. (2011). Do multi-view X-ray systems improve X-ray image interpretation in airport security screening? *Zeitschrift für Arbeitswissenschaft*, 65(3), 166–173.

Zentai, G. (2010). X-ray imaging for homeland security. *International Journal of Signal and Imaging Systems Engineering*, 3(1), 13–20.

Chapter 4

Software-based personal identity verification technologies

4.1 INTRODUCTION

Person identification technologies used by law enforcement agencies include a variety of tools developed for security and law enforcement purposes.

Portable Devices: Law enforcement agencies often use portable devices in field operations to conduct identity queries. These devices can quickly verify identity by scanning ID cards or driver's licenses.

Biometric Recognition: Biometric technologies, such as fingerprint scanners, facial recognition cameras, or iris scanners, provide fast and reliable authentication using the physical characteristics of individuals. A fingerprint is a unique and difficult-to-forge biometric data. Since the 1960s, fingerprint recognition systems have made great advances in software and hardware. Especially thanks to the development of inkless fingerprint scanners and increases in processing power, fingerprint recognition technology is not only limited to detecting criminals but also widely used in civil security applications such as access control, attendance monitoring, and computer user login (Sönmez Battini, Özbek & Özbek, 2000).

Databases: Law enforcement agencies have access to databases containing information on criminals and suspects. These databases contain information such as personal details, criminal history, and photographs.

Mobile Applications: Law enforcement officers can make identity inquiries through mobile applications in the field. These applications allow real-time data sharing.

Fast Number Plate Recognition: Cameras that automatically identify vehicle number plates can instantly identify the owners and past records of vehicles.

These technologies assist law enforcement agencies in authentication, crime detection, and security. However, privacy and data protection issues related to the use of these technologies should also be considered.

4.2 LEGAL LEGISLATION

The legal framework that applies to law enforcement's use of person identification technologies is of paramount importance.

 DOI: 10.1201/9781003597445-4

Constitution and Fundamental Rights: Fundamental rights such as personal privacy, freedom of expression, and fair trial are important elements to be considered in the use of technology.

Personal Data Protection Laws: Many countries have personal data protection laws that include rules on the collection, processing, storage, and sharing of personal data. It is an important development that genetic and biometric information is recognized as sensitive data separately from health data in recently adopted data protection laws (Cemil, 2011).

Anti-crime Laws: Law enforcement agencies may have special powers to fight crime. However, these powers are generally limited by law and fair process, and evidence must be obtained.

Telecommunications Laws: The monitoring of communications data, such as mobile phone signals, internet traffic, etc., is governed by telecommunications laws.

Law Enforcement Laws: Law enforcement agencies usually have their own specific laws, and their powers and responsibilities are regulated by these laws.

Court Orders: The use of identity interrogation technologies may be based on court orders or search warrants.

These legal provisions reflect the need for law enforcement agencies to comply with the law and respect the fundamental rights of individuals when using identity interrogation technologies. It is particularly important to analyze the laws of the country concerned, as they may differ by country and region.

Databases used by law enforcement agencies are critical tools for crime detection, investigations, and general security. It is a fact that technological developments in criminal justice systems date back to the mid-1980s and that law enforcement agencies created their profile databases in the 1990s. Initially, these databases contained only DNA profiles of convicted rapists and murderers. However, the success of these databases in solving violent crimes has created a momentum that Congress and state legislatures are considering expanding with a critical eye (Rothstein & Talbott, 2006). These databases support the effective work of law enforcement by storing a variety of information.

Offence Information and History: Law enforcement agencies can examine the criminal history of offenders using databases containing their past offences and sentences. This information helps in the investigation and criminal sanction processes.

Credentials: Identification information contains information on crime suspects and witnesses. This information is used to take the statements of witnesses before or after arriving at the scene of the crime.

Vehicle License Plates and Records: Vehicle number plates and records are used to detect traffic violations and to track stolen vehicles.

Identity Verification and Search Warrants: Law enforcement agencies may consult databases to verify the validity of legal documents such as search warrants or arrest warrants. As a result of routine biometric checks, around 20–25 suspects are arrested every week (Mansfield-Devine, 2012).

Fingerprint and DNA Data: Fingerprints or DNA samples found at crime scenes can be recorded in databases and associated with past crimes. The prevailing view among law enforcement officials is that the more profiles in a database, the more likely a profile is to match evidence found at a crime scene (Rothstein & Talbott, 2006).

Monitoring and Intelligence Information: Intelligence data and surveillance information can also be stored in databases within the scope of combating threats, criminal organizations, or terrorism. Biometric information plays an important role not only in authentication but also in creating a detailed intelligence table by combining data from multiple sources (Mansfield-Devine, 2012).

Mobile Phone and Internet Traces: Telecommunication and internet traces can be monitored to detect criminal activities and communications.

While these databases help law enforcement agencies to work more effectively, data security and privacy issues need to be considered at the same time. It is important to protect personal data, take into account legal limitations, and to prevent the use of databases for purposes other than legal ones.

4.3 PERSON IDENTITY INQUIRY VIA RADIO TABLET

Mobile applications used by law enforcement agencies are tools that help these agencies to carry out their fieldwork more effectively and efficiently. These applications are used for purposes such as security, crime detection, data sharing, and communication.

Authentication and Search Warrant Inquiry: Mobile applications help law enforcement officers to perform identity verification procedures quickly. The mobile vehicle inquiry system was developed to provide authorities with information about vehicles, individuals, or events through mobile computers and personal digital assistants. This system allows authorities to query driver, vehicle, and identity information online over GPRS (Kula & Guler, 2016). It can also be used to verify the validity of legal documents such as search warrants.

Crime Scene Reports: Law enforcement agencies can create instant reports at the scene of a crime and document the details of the crime scene with pictures and notes.

Ticketing and Traffic Violations: Mobile applications can be used to issue traffic fines or detect traffic violations.

Current Database Access: Mobile applications provide law enforcement agencies with access to up-to-date databases in the field. They can instantly access information such as criminal history, missing persons, or stolen vehicles.

Intelligence Sharing: Law enforcement officers can instantly share intelligence information with other team members or units.

Geolocation Tracking: Tracking the geographical location of law enforcement units or vehicles can be used for tracking and cooperation purposes.

Reporting and Statistics: Applications can generate reports on law enforcement operations and track statistics such as crime rates, successes, and needs.

Team Communication: Mobile applications are used for instant communication between team members. Instant messaging, video chat, and voice communication can be used for this purpose.

These mobile applications enable law enforcement officers to work more effectively and faster in the field. However, issues such as data security, confidentiality, and compliance with legal regulations should be carefully considered.

Handheld devices are tools that help law enforcement officers to carry out identity inquiries quickly and effectively in the field. These devices are generally mobile devices that law enforcement officers carry on their persons or in their vehicles.

Smartphones and Tablets: Law enforcement officers can conduct identity inquiries through smartphones and tablets. They can obtain information by scanning ID cards, driving licenses, or passports through these devices, applications, and cameras. It is stated that mobile technology is one of the most common areas of use in law enforcement operations (Dasher, 2016).

Hand Terminal Devices: Specially designed handheld terminal devices have the ability to access databases by quickly scanning ID cards or documents. These devices are generally designed to be durable and suitable for field conditions.

Portable Barcode and RFID Readers: Barcodes or RFID chips on ID documents can be read through portable readers. The new generation of ID cards is considered secure smart cards and uses a public key infrastructure. These cards allow data to be digitally signed electronically. The signing process, which is performed by means of a smart card reader and application programming interface, prevents forgery and increases data security while maintaining data integrity (Küçük, 2019). In this way, identity information can be quickly detected.

Near Field Communication (NFC) Technology: NFC technology enables fast data sharing by using smart cards or identity documents. In this way, identity information can be obtained instantly.

Data Connectivity and Internet Access: Portable devices can usually access the internet via a mobile data connection or Wi-Fi. This allows instant access to up-to-date databases.

Camera and Photo Capture: Portable devices can take and save photos of people through integrated cameras. These photos can be used for identification and the identification of criminals.

These portable devices provide great convenience to law enforcement officers in fieldwork. They are used for fast data access, sharing up-to-date information, and effective authentication. However, data security, confidentiality, and observance of legal regulations are important in the use of these devices.

4.4 BIOMETRIC RECOGNITION TECHNOLOGIES

Biometric identification is a science and technique for recognizing human characteristics, both physiological and behavioral. Person authentication based on biometric verification is becoming increasingly popular in various applications such as banking, aviation, financial transactions, etc. (Gaur, Shah, & Thakker, 2012). Law enforcement agencies use biometric recognition technologies for authentication and recognition using unique physical or behavioral characteristics of individuals. These technologies play an important role in security and law enforcement.

Fingerprint Recognition: Fingerprints are unique thanks to the skin folds and marks on the fingertips of each individual. Fingerprint scanners identify a person by reading their fingerprint. But now, fingerprints can offer much more information. Particularly noteworthy are advances in fingerprint technology that can simultaneously provide personal information such as the drugs consumed, explosives used, and even a person's chemical profile (Hazarika & Russell, 2012). This technology provides authentication in a fast and reliable way.

Face Recognition: Face recognition identifies a person's identity by analyzing their facial features. Face recognition systems generally use the spatial relationship between the positions of facial features such as eyes, nose, lips, chin, and the general appearance of the face. Face scanning is done through camera systems, and authentication is performed using the unique features of the face. Although face recognition technologies have advantages such as being non-intrusive, high user acceptance, and providing good recognition performance in controlled environments, they continue to face challenges due to factors such as lighting conditions or different angles of the face (Jain & Kumar, 2012). Therefore, there are still some important challenges for the development and application of face recognition technology.

Iris Recognition: The iris of the eye is the colored annular area surrounding the pupil. Iris patterns are unique. No two irises are the same, even if a person has a right and left eye (Gaur, Shah & Thakker, 2012). Iris scanners perform authentication by scanning and recording these patterns. Iris recognition has been integrated into many large-scale personal identification systems. The border crossing system in the United Arab Emirates is one example. Various efforts are also being made for remote capture of the iris (Jain & Kumar, 2012). It is a biometric recognition method that provides very high reliability.

Voice Recognition: Identification can be made using voice tone, speech rate, and other voice features. The movement of the lips, jaws, tongue, pitch, and larynx constitute the behavioral component of the voice and may change over time depending on the age and medical condition of the person (e.g., colds) (Jain & Kumar, 2012). Therefore, this method may be less reliable than other biometric technologies.

These biometric recognition technologies are generally used in fieldwork and security control of law enforcement organizations. However, data security and privacy issues should be considered. It is important that personal data is protected and used in accordance with legal requirements.

4.5 NUMBER PLATE IDENTIFICATION SYSTEMS

Number plate recognition uses image processing and character recognition approaches to identify vehicles by automatically reading their number plates (Lekhana & Srikantaswamy, 2012).

Automatic number plate recognition (ANPR) technologies used by law enforcement agencies are vehicle number plate reading systems capable of automatically detecting, recognizing, and recording the number plates of vehicles. Since number plate detection is of great importance, various algorithms have been developed for this purpose. The license plate recognition process generally involves two main mechanisms, namely license plate detection (LPD) followed by license plate identification (LPI) (Wafy & Madbouly, 2016). This technology is used in many areas such as traffic control, security, crime detection, and anti-smuggling.

The features of fast number plate recognition technologies are presented below.

Working Principle: Fast number plate recognition systems display and read the number plates of vehicles using cameras and optical character recognition (OCR) software. The letters and numbers on the plate are recognized by the OCR software and converted into numerical data. Edge statistics and mathematical morphology-based methods for license plate region detection give very effective results. These methods work by calculating features such as gradient magnitude and local variance in the image. In particular, they use these features because the brightness changes in the license plate region are more pronounced and frequent than in other regions. In addition, block-based processing methods also support this approach (Anagnostopoulos et al. 2006)

Camera Positioning: The system works with cameras that are usually mounted on the roadside or at traffic points, and it has been determined that it is not possible to read license plates from any distance, and it is not suitable to be used only at a certain distance in a place that is set and fixed (Çelik & Erdoğan, 2021). These cameras monitor the road travelled by vehicles and scan the number plates.

Database Comparison: The scanned license plate information is compared with previously created vehicle license plate databases. The number plates of the vehicles arriving at the inspection point must be read using image processing techniques and recorded in a database with time and date information. It also aims to calculate the time difference between the last time the vehicle was viewed and the current date, and to use this information to determine whether the vehicle needs to be checked again within the specified time period. In addition, if a suspicious or reported vehicle license plate is entered into the database, it will be possible to ensure that the relevant vehicle is stopped despite the intensity of the inspection by warning the personnel in charge (Çelik & Erdoğan, 2021). Stolen vehicles, vehicles with violations, or other security risks can be recorded in these databases.

Instant Warning and Processing: The display time of the number plate read instantly from the number plates saved in the database is taken, and the time difference between this information and the previous display date is calculated. If the detected vehicle license plate has never been displayed before, "displaying for the first time" information is given. If the detected vehicle license plate has been previously recognized as a suspicious vehicle, "suspicious vehicle information" is displayed; otherwise, a "-" sign is displayed indicating that the vehicle is not suspicious (Çelik & Erdoğan, 2021). If any discrepancy is detected in the license plate, the system can quickly alert law enforcement agencies. It can also identify situations such as traffic violations or wanted vehicles.

Real-Time Tracking: The system can track the movement of vehicles instantaneously. This is especially used to capture wanted vehicles and crime suspects. Real-time number plate recognition algorithms usually consist of four processing steps: Image acquisition, number plate detection and extraction, character segmentation through a combination of spectral analysis and connected component analysis, and character recognition using support vector machines (Lekhana & Srikantaswamy, 2012).

Traffic Analysis and Statistics: The Rapid number plate recognition system can be used for traffic management and planning by collecting data such as traffic density analysis and traffic flow monitoring. Considering the needs of public safety management and increasing traffic complexity, number plate recognition technology is of great importance. It enables fast information access over the communication network, facilitates remote data retrieval at any time, and is thus highly favorable for traffic safety supervision and monitoring. Moreover, the automatic combination of IoT and number plate recognition technology contributes greatly to the acquisition of real-time road conditions and has the potential to improve overall traffic information [16].

Security Controls: It can also be used in places where security checks are carried out, such as airports, harbors, or border crossing points, to monitor and evaluate vehicles. Especially the 11 September terrorist attacks led governments to invest in surveillance technologies to protect their citizens against horrific attacks. To prevent such attacks, law enforcement agencies have started to make extensive use of surveillance systems, mainly CCTV, to monitor human activity in areas such as airports, harbors, borders, and crowded city streets (Ren et al. 2012).

REFERENCES

Anagnostopoulos, C. N. E., Anagnostopoulos, I. E., Loumos, V., & Kayafas, E. (2006). A license plate-recognition algorithm for intelligent transportation system applications. *IEEE Transactions on Intelligent Transportation Systems*, 7(3), 377–392.

Çelik, R., & Erdoğan, K. (2021). Kolluk Kuvvetleri Tarafından Yapılan Araç Denetimlerindeki Verimliliğinin Artırılmasını Amaçlayan Plaka Tanıma Sistemi. *Avrupa Bilim ve Teknoloji Dergisi, 30*, 62–65

Cemil, K. (2011). Avrupa birliği veri koruma direktifi ekseninde hassas (kişisel) veriler ve işlenmesi. *Journal of Istanbul University Law Faculty, 69*(1–2), 317–334.

Dasher, A. D. (2016). Technology distractions on patrol: Giving police officers a voice (Doctoral dissertation, Walden University).

Gaur, S., Shah, V. A., & Thakker, M. (2012). Biometric recognition techniques: A review. *International Journal of Advanced Research in Electrical, Electronics and Instrumentation Engineering, 1*(4), 282–290.

Hazarika, P., & Russell, D. A. (2012). Advances in fingerprint analysis. *Angewandte Chemie International Edition, 51*(15), 3524–3531.

Jain, A. K., & Kumar, A. (2012). Biometric recognition: An overview. In E. Mordini & D. Tzovaras (Eds.), *Second Generation Biometrics: The Ethical, Legal and Social Context*, 49–79. Springer.

Küçük, K. (2019). Güvenilir işletim ortamı teknolojisi kullanılarak mobil kimlik uygulaması geliştirilmesi (Master's thesis, TOBB University of Economics and Technology, Graduate School of Engineering and Science).

Kula, S., & Guler, A. (2016). Smart public safety: Application of mobile electronic system integration (MOBESE) in Istanbul. Smarter as the new urban agenda: A comprehensive view of the 21st century city, 243–258.

Lekhana, G. C., & Srikantaswamy, R. (2012). Real time license plate recognition system. *International Journal of Advanced Technology & Engineering Research, 2*(4), 5–9.

Mansfield-Devine, S. (2012). Biometrics at war: The US military's need for identification and authentication. *Biometric Technology Today, 2012*(5), 5–8.

Ren, X., Jiang, H., Wu, Y., Yang, X., & Liu, K. (2012, October). The Internet of Things in the license plate recognition technology application and design. In 2012 Second International Conference on Business Computing and Global Informatization (pp. 969–972). IEEE.

Rothstein, M. A., & Talbott, M. K. (2006). The expanding use of DNA in law enforcement: What role for privacy?. *Journal of Law, Medicine & Ethics, 34*(2), 153–164.

Sönmez Battini, E., Özbek, N. Ö., & Özbek, Ö. (2000). *Avuç izi ve Parmak İzine Dayalı Bir Biyometrik Tanıma Sistemi.* İstanbul Bilgi Üniversitesi, Bilgisayar Bilimleri Bölümü, İstanbul.

Wafy, M., & Madbouly, A. M. (2016). Efficient method for vehicle license plate identification based on learning a morphological feature. *IET Intelligent Transport Systems, 10*(6), 389–395.

Chapter 5

Hardware-based communication technologies

5.1 INTRODUCTION

Rapid developments in technology offer the opportunity to increase the potential for interaction with other people by contributing to the ability to communicate. Developing technologies open the door to different communication methods (Sönmez Battini, Özbek & Özbek, 2000).

Communication technologies used by law enforcement agencies facilitate security, emergency management, field coordination, and communication. These technologies accelerate communication between teams and enable more effective operations. The communication technologies used by law enforcement agencies are presented below with subheadings.

Radio Communication: Law enforcement officers can communicate instantly using radios or radio devices. These devices provide fast communication, especially between field teams. Law enforcement officers coordinate using these devices during emergencies or operations.

Mobile Communication Devices: Devices such as portable radios or mobile phones enable law enforcement officers to communicate in the field. Especially, mobile applications and instant messaging strengthen the communication of the teams.

Data Communication: Systems that enable instant data sharing between law enforcement vehicles and field teams are used. These systems are used in vehicle license plate control, identity verification, and other data sharing processes.

GPS and Location Tracking: GPS technology helps law enforcement agencies track teams and determine their locations. This is important for emergencies or coordinating operations.

Video and Image Communication: Using instant video and image communication technologies, law enforcement officers can remotely inspect crime scenes and video chat with other team members.

Data Encryption and Security: The security of the data used during communication is of great importance. Encryption technologies ensure that data is protected from unauthorized access.

DOI: 10.1201/9781003597445-5

Integrated Communication Centers: Law enforcement emergency centers or central command centers manage communication between teams and ensure coordination. These centers route incoming calls, assess emergencies, and direct field teams.

These communication technologies enable law enforcement agencies to communicate quickly and effectively, manage operations, and ensure security. Communication technology meets an important need of humanity as a rapidly developing and increasingly complex field. The demands in this field are increasing day by day and it is becoming increasingly difficult to meet these demands. Among these demands, factors such as high performance, small size, wide bandwidth, and low cost are particularly prominent. In communication systems, especially in sensitive receiver circuits, the use of bandpass radio frequency (RF) filters is a critical requirement to isolate the desired signal from all signals outside the operating band (Belen, Gülseren & Güneş, 2018).

5.2 NARROWBAND COMMUNICATION SYSTEMS

Nowadays, intensive research continues on communication systems in order to improve the quality of data communication. For this reason, antenna design studies with different properties are developing rapidly to improve the quality of communication in military and civil applications. In particular, many applications of microwave technology are successfully realized with the use of metamaterials (Belen, Gülseren & Güneş, 2018).

Narrowband communication technologies refer to systems that provide communication with low bandwidth. These technologies involve communication systems that perform data communication in certain frequency ranges and generally have low data rates. Narrowband communication systems provide advantages such as long-distance communication, low energy consumption, and stronger signal penetration.

Areas of Use: Narrowband communication technologies are used in industrial automation, remote monitoring, the Internet of Things (IoT), smart agriculture, healthcare, energy management, and many other fields. It is especially preferred for communication in remote areas or harsh conditions.

Frequency Ranges: Narrowband communication usually operates in low-frequency ranges. This frequency range increases the communication distance while keeping energy consumption low.

Energy Efficiency: Narrowband technologies generally provide energy-efficient operation. They are evaluated to process relatively smaller-sized messages. Sending less data will trigger less energy consumption and therefore means longer battery life (Baloğlu & Karademiroğlu, 2019) For this reason, they can offer long battery life in devices running on batteries.

Long Range: Low bandwidth can provide longer communication distances. This feature facilitates the communication of devices in remote areas with centralized systems.

Strong Signal Penetration: Narrowband signals are capable of stronger penetration against obstructions and walls. This can maintain communication even in confined spaces or areas with obstacles.

Data Rate: Narrowband communication systems can offer lower data rates compared to technologies with high data rates. They operate in the publicly available 200 kHz band to exchange messages using narrowband modulation. Each message is 100 Hz wide, and depending on the region, data transfer rates of 100 or 600 bits per second are achieved (Baloğlu & Karademiroğlu, 2019). However, such technologies are particularly suitable for applications where low data flow rates are needed.

Wireless Sensor Networks: Narrowband communication technologies are wireless communication technologies developed to connect a wide range of devices and services using cellular telecommunication bands. NB-IoT is one of a set of mobile IoT (Internet of Things) infrastructures standardized by 3GPP (Baloğlu & Karademiroğlu, 2019). Wireless sensor networks may prefer narrowband technologies for data collection and communication.

In summary, narrowband communication technologies offer advantages such as energy efficiency, long range and strong signal penetration, and are particularly used in areas such as remote monitoring, IoT, and industrial automation.

Law enforcement agencies often use narrowband communication technologies in areas such as field operations, security applications, and emergency management. These technologies offer energy efficiency, long range and strong penetration features by providing communication with low bandwidth.

IoT Applications: Law enforcement agencies can manage smart city applications using Internet of Things (IoT) technologies. They can use narrowband communications to collect data from devices such as the status of streetlights, traffic signals, and environmental sensors.

Remote Monitoring and Control: Law enforcement agencies can monitor security cameras and other sensors using remote monitoring and control systems. Narrowband technologies can help them monitor site status by providing reliable communication even over long distances.

Emergency Communication: Narrowband communications are used for emergency and disaster management. Especially in cases where the communication infrastructure is weakened or damaged, these technologies are preferred to maintain communication.

Environmental Monitoring and Sensing: Narrowband technologies can be used in environmental monitoring applications such as air quality monitoring, radiation levels, and fire detection.

Portable Devices: Law enforcement agencies can transmit data from the field to central systems using narrowband communication technologies through portable devices. In this way, instant status updates can be provided.

Data Security: Narrowband communication technologies provide secure communication supported by data security measures. Measures such as data encryption and authentication are used.

Energy Efficiency: Such communication technologies offer energy-efficient operation. This feature is important in extending the battery life of portable devices and long-term field operations.

Law enforcement agencies can manage operations more effectively by using narrowband communication technologies, especially in remote monitoring, emergency management, and IoT applications.

Digital radio system refers to a digital radio communication system designed for secure communications used by law enforcement agencies. DMR stands for "digital mobile radio" and is a standard for digital radio communication. It is an unregistered digital radio standard created by the European Telecommunications Standards Institute (ETSI) and supported by different radio equipment manufacturers, as well as open source developers and radio amateurs (Fongen, 2022). This system aims to meet the communication needs of law enforcement personnel such as gendarmerie, police, security forces, and emergency teams in a secure and effective manner. Some of the features of the DMR digital radio system are listed below.

Digital Communication: Thanks to digital technology, voice communication becomes clearer and more understandable. It offers better sound quality compared to traditional analog radio systems.

Data and Voice Communication: The DMR system can support not only voice communication but also text-based messaging and data transfer. To transmit IPv4 packets over the radio, a 96-bit header is added, containing information such as the DMR IDs of the sender and receiver, the type of transmission, and an acknowledgement request. The IPv4 packet is sent divided into this header block and the last block is padded for correction while a 32-bit CRC check is added at the same time. Each block is encoded with a 196-bit Turbo Encoding. This Turbo Coded block carries a total of 264 bits of data, adding the synchronization and signalling fields. The transmission type can be observed in the signalling field before the entire code is decoded. When an IPv4 packet is sent to a DMR unit, special IPv4 addresses derived from the DMR IDs of the sending and receiving units are used. In addition, a special IPv4 address is set for multicast (Fongen, 2022).

Encrypted Communication: The system ensures the security of communication by using special encryption methods. This makes it difficult for third parties to listen or interfere.

Integration Capability: DMR radio systems can be integrated with different platforms and communication devices. This increases coordination.

Group and Private Conversations: It offers the ability to communicate in different groups or between individual users.

Emergency and Alerts: The DMR radio system makes it easy to facilitate critical communications, such as emergency calls and alerts.

Such encrypted digital radio systems support security and emergency teams to communicate effectively and conduct their operations more efficiently. Secure and reliable communications are critical for law enforcement organizations to conduct successful operations.

5.3 BROADBAND COMMUNICATION SYSTEMS (LTE)

Broadband communication technologies refer to systems that provide communication with high bandwidth. These technologies include large data transfer, high-speed internet access, and operation in wider frequency ranges. In the last few years, interest in ultra-wideband communication systems has been growing rapidly. These systems use very short duration pulses instead of conventional sinusoidal carrier modulation to transmit information [5]. Law enforcement agencies can use broadband communication technologies for fast data transmission, field coordination, and security purposes.

LTE systems have a number of potential advantages such as high data rates, low risk of interference and detection, simple system design, economical cost, reduced average power consumption, and low sensitivity to the near-far problem (Elbahhar, Rivenq-Menhaj & Rouvaen, 2005).

LTE technology is efficiently used in wireless broadband communications for mobile devices. It provides flexible bandwidth and frequency with high speed and peak data rates. Optimizing resource allocation is vital to improve the performance of the LTE system and meet the user's quality of service (QoS) needs (Ahmed et al., 2023)

Data Rate and Capacity: Broadband technologies offer high data rates. This means the ability to quickly transmit large amounts of data. This is ideal for quickly transferring videos, images, and other types of large data.

High-Speed Internet: Broadband technologies provide fast internet access, enabling teams to quickly receive data and communicate from the field. This enables operations to be managed more effectively.

Enhanced Audio and Video Communications: High bandwidth enables high-quality audio and video communications. This is beneficial in applications such as video chat, video monitoring, and live streaming.

Application Diversity: Broadband technologies support a range of applications. This can include mobile applications, data collection sensors, remote monitoring systems, and more.

Remote Management and Control: Law enforcement agencies can create remote monitoring, control, and management systems with broadband communication technologies. This can include applications such as monitoring security cameras, managing traffic signals, or managing emergencies.

Data Security: Broadband communication systems can include various security measures to ensure data security even during high-speed data transfer.

Mobile Applications: Broadband technologies enable mobile applications to run quickly and effectively. This allows field officers to quickly access up-to-date data via portable devices.

Law enforcement agencies can utilize broadband communication technologies for fast data transmission, high-quality audio/video communications, and overall operational efficiency. UWB radios, which have an extremely wide transmission bandwidth and operate with low transmission power, offer inherent privacy features. They are also being evaluated for military networks due to their low detection and interference capabilities (Chiani & Giorgetti, 2009). These technologies can be an important tool to provide faster, more secure, and more effective communication.

LTE is a wireless communication technology known by the acronym "Long-Term Evolution". In the mobile communications industry, it is also referred to as a 4G network. LTE is a communications standard designed to provide high-speed data transmission, low latency, and improved wireless connectivity.

High Data Rates: LTE technology enables high-speed data transfer. This means faster performance in activities such as video streaming, file downloading, and web browsing.

Low Latency: LTE supports real-time applications with low latency. This is important in applications such as online gaming, voice, and video calls.

Large Capacity: The LTE network is designed to support large amounts of data traffic. This ensures good performance even in congested areas.

Packet Switching: LTE breaks data into small packets and transmits these packets over the network, transferring data more efficiently.

Advanced Modulation and Multiple Input-Output (MIMO): Advanced modulation techniques and MIMO enable support for more simultaneous connections while increasing data rates.

IP-Based Networks: LTE uses an internet protocol (IP)-based network structure. This provides greater compatibility and flexibility.

LTE technology is considered a major advance in wireless communications. The 4G network offers higher speeds, lower latency, and large capacity than the earlier 3G technology. LTE infrastructure enables the connection of a range of devices such as smartphones, tablets, mobile devices, and even IoT (Internet of Things) devices.

5.4 STRINGED SYSTEMS

Wire communication systems used by law enforcement agencies are communication infrastructures that are generally used for special or specific purposes. These systems transmit data through cables or wires.

Telephone Lines: Traditional telephone lines provide voice communication. Law enforcement agencies may use telephone lines for emergencies or important communications.

Data Lines: Law enforcement agencies can use data lines to share information and data. In particular, data lines can be used to connect with centralized systems or to access databases.

Wired Networks: Law enforcement agencies can set up indoor or outdoor networks through cabling. This may include connection of surveillance cameras, data transfer, or inter-office communication.

Emergency Systems: Emergency systems used in buildings or facilities can transmit fire alarms, security alarms, or emergency calls via cabling.

Security Systems: Security systems establish wired communication with components such as security cameras, door access control systems, and alarm systems.

Voice Communications: Law enforcement agencies can provide voice communication with teams in the field by establishing wired communication with central communication centers or command centers.

Fiber Optic Infrastructures: Fiber optic cables provide high-speed data transfer and can offer reliable communication over long distances. Therefore, fiber optic infrastructures can be used for important data transfers and network connections.

Wired Vehicle Communications: Communication systems used in law enforcement vehicles generally provide in-vehicle and out-of-vehicle communications via cabling.

Wired communication systems can offer advantages in terms of reliability and data security. However, disadvantages such as limited mobility and installation costs should also be considered.

The term 'Secure VoIP Phone' can refer to VoIP (Voice over Internet Protocol) phones—a voice communication technology designed to provide secure communication. Nowadays, mobile communications are evolving from Global System for Mobile Communications (GSM) and Code Division Multiple Access (CDMA) mechanisms to internet-enabled communication technologies. In GSM and CDMA technology, mobile phone users have to be connected to local service providers. Experienced criminals are also aware of law enforcement tactics for GSM/CDMA-based call investigations. VoIP is a voice over internet protocol, which is an internet-based calling mechanism. VoIP is an internet-based calling service, which is one of the solutions used by sophisticated criminals to hide themselves from the ordinary communication mechanism (Singh & Chaudhary, 2023). Secure VoIP phones are designed to perform this communication in a more secure and protected manner.

Data Encryption: Secure VoIP phones provide protection against eavesdropping by encrypting voice data during communication.

Authentication: May include security measures that require users to verify their identity. This reduces the risk of unauthorized access.

Security Protocols: Secure VoIP phones can use special security protocols and algorithms to ensure secure communication.

Emergency Management: Some models may offer special buttons or functions for emergencies, enabling quick emergency calls.

Data Protection: Secure VoIP phones can use strict data protection methods to reduce the risk of data breaches.

Ease of Use: They often offer a similar user interface to traditional phones, so users can easily adapt.

Secure VoIP phones are used especially in areas where security and sensitive information communication are required, such as government agencies, the defense sector, emergency centers, and similar places. These phones meet the need to provide secure communications, increasing data confidentiality and communication security.

5.5 MIXING AND BLINDING SYSTEMS

Jamming and jamming communication systems are specialized technologies used especially for security purposes. A visual of a corrupted signal is presented in Figure 5.1.

Jamming Systems: Jammers are devices used to prevent or interrupt the normal operation of targeted devices or communication systems. They generally aim to interrupt communication by filling the signals on radio frequencies or other communication channels with noise or random signals. Law enforcement or military units may use jammers to take measures against terrorist attacks, intercept illegal communications, or support security operations.

Signal jammers are used to block or jam communication or control signals in the targeted frequency range. By generating noise or random signals in certain bands of the radio frequency spectrum, they aim to block or interrupt the communication of target devices. They can be used by security teams to protect against terrorist attacks or illegal activities. They can be used in military operations to intercept or disrupt the enemy's communication. However, there are also systems that counter these jammers. These are also called anti-interference systems. In a conventional anti-jamming system, a transmitter that wants to send a signal to a single receiver spreads its signal power over a wide frequency spectrum to stop the jammer from interfering with the transmission (Desmedt et al., 2001).

Anti-drone Systems: The rapid expansion of the drone industry has exceeded regulations for safe and secure drone operations, making them representative tools of illegal and subversive terrorism and crime (Park et al., 2021). Anti-drone systems are used against unmanned aerial vehicles (drones). These systems are designed to prevent or neutralize drones from entering airspace or conducting their activities. Such systems can work by methods such as detecting, tracking, jamming, or guiding drones.

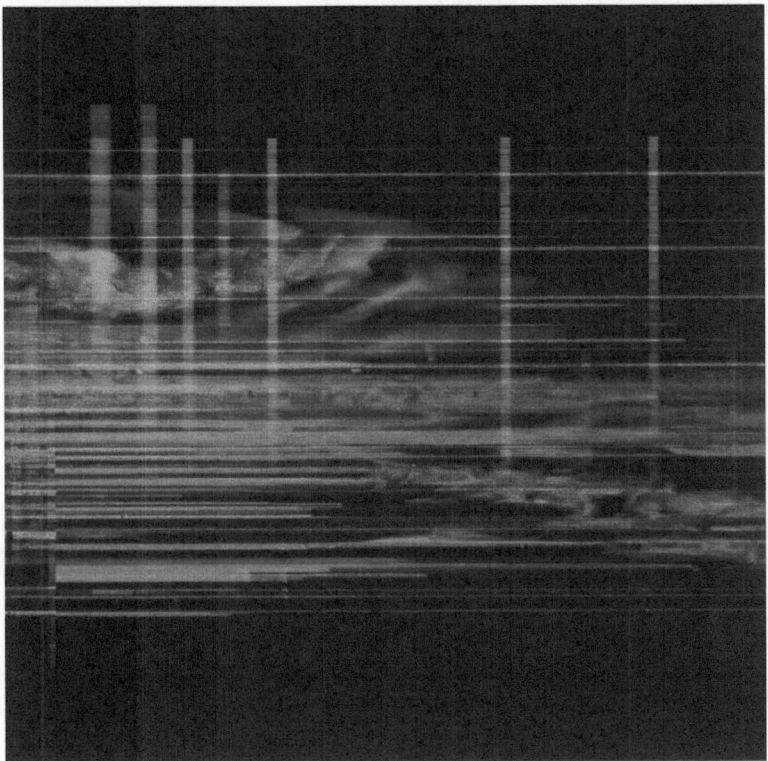

Figure 5.1 Corrupted signal image

Anti-drone systems are designed to protect against unmanned aerial vehicles (drones). They use various methods to detect, track, intercept, or control drones. Drone detection is performed using different characteristics of flying drones. Drones usually emit heat, sound, and radio frequency (RF) signals to communicate with the remote operator. The detection system collects sensor data to verify the presence of drones in nearby areas. Based on these measurements, it can determine the expected locations of drones (Park et al., 2021). It provides security by using it in airports, military bases, event areas, and other sensitive areas.

Spoofing Systems: Spoofing systems aim to manipulate the normal functioning of target devices or systems. For example, GPS spoofing systems can mimic the GPS signal of a target device, causing it to receive false location information. Such systems may be used for security operations or defense purposes.

Jamming systems aim to achieve undesirable results by manipulating the normal functioning of target devices. GPS jamming systems can spoof the position of the target device by mimicking GPS signals. The performance of GPS receivers is severely degraded when jamming sources exceed the anti-jamming capability of the system. Among different jamming sources, continuous wave interference (CWI) and pulsed CWI have been shown to have serious effects on the quality of the received GPS signal (Chien, 2013). Such systems can mislead navigation systems, misdirecting devices to the wrong location or putting them in an undesirable situation. They can be used in areas such as defense purposes, cybersecurity testing, and research.

REFERENCES

Ahmed, F. Y., Masli, A. A., Khassawneh, B., Yousif, J. H., & Zebari, D. A. (2023). Optimized downlink scheduling over LTE network based on artificial neural network. *Computers, 12*(9), 179.

Baloğlu, A., & Karademiroğlu, O. (2019). Akıllı şehirlerde kablosuz haberleşme teknolojileri ve doğru teknoloji seçimi. *İstanbul Sabahattin Zaim Üniversitesi fen bilimleri enstitüsü dergisi, 1*(1), 22–29.

Belen, M. A., Gülseren, A. H., & Güneş, F. (2018, May). Narrow dual band frequency selective surface design for X-band application. In *2018 26th Signal Processing and Communications Applications Conference (SIU)* (pp. 1–4). IEEE.

Chiani, M., & Giorgetti, A. (2009). Coexistence between UWB and narrow-band wireless communication systems. *Proceedings of the IEEE, 97*(2), 231–254.

Chien, Y. R. (2013). Design of GPS anti-jamming systems using adaptive notch filters. *IEEE Systems Journal, 9*(2), 451–460.

Desmedt, Y., Safavi-Naini, R., Wang, H., Batten, L., Charnes, C., & Pieprzyk, J. (2001). Broadcast anti-jamming systems. *Computer Networks, 35*(2–3), 223–236.

Elbahhar, F., Rivenq-Menhaj, A., & Rouvaen, J. M. (2005). Multi-user ultra-wide band communication system based on modified gegenbauer and hermite functions. *Wireless Personal Communications, 34*, 255–277.

Fongen, A. (2022) Integration of digital mobile radio in a sensor network. The Sixteenth International Conference on Sensor Technologies and Applications, ISBN: 978-1-68558-005-65.

Park, S., Kim, H. T., Lee, S., Joo, H., & Kim, H. (2021). Survey on anti-drone systems: Components, designs, and challenges. *IEEE Access, 9*, 42635–42659.

Singh, I., & Chaudhary, N. K. (2023). A study on methodology on VoIP-based communication investigation through network packet analysis. *Int. J. Electronic Security and Digital Forensics, 15*(5), 443.

Sönmez Battini, E., Özbek, N. Ö., & Özbek, Ö. (2000). *Avuç izi ve Parmak İzine Dayalı Bir Biyometrik Tanıma Sistemi.* İstanbul Bilgi Üniversitesi, Bilgisayar Bilimleri Bölümü, İstanbul.

Chapter 6

Critical technologies based on software or embedded systems

6.1 INTRODUCTION

Today's trending technologies are of great importance in the rapidly developing digital world and have an impact on many sectors. These technologies shape today's rapid digital transformation and shape the future. Companies, organizations, and industries try to gain a competitive advantage and adapt to the rapidly changing world by following these trending technologies.

6.2 GLOBAL POSITIONING SYSTEMS (GNSS)

Global positioning systems (GNSS) are technologies used to provide positioning and time synchronization across the globe. Basically, these systems use signals from one or more satellite networks to determine the user's location.

GNSS, best known as GPS (Global Positioning System), is commonly referred to as a satellite navigation or satellite positioning system. GPS is a space-based positioning, navigation, and timing system developed by the US Department of Defense (DoD). It originated in the late 1960s and early 1970s as a merger of synergistic Navy and Air Force programs for timing and space-based navigation, respectively (McNeff, 2002). Other GNSS systems include Russia's GLONASS, the European Union's Galileo and China's Beidou.

These systems send continuous signals from satellite orbits to the Earth's surface. The devices receive these signals and calculate the distance and time between each satellite. Using this data, the devices can determine the user's 3D location (latitude, longitude, and altitude).

Common uses of GNSS technology include navigation, geographic information systems (GIS), military applications, air and maritime transportation, agriculture, weather forecasting, and emergency management.

The GNSS system is a precise and efficient positioning technology that is widely used around the world. In addition to determining the user's current position, the system also provides speed, direction, and time information.

DOI: 10.1201/9781003597445-6

The most common uses of GNSS include the following: Navigation in activities such as hiking and geocaching, navigation of vehicles and other vehicles, ocean navigation and channel scanning for marine vessels, and aircraft control such as approaching and landing at airports. Some more sensitive applications may require carrier phase measurements. GNSS is also used for tracking people, vehicles, and ships (Langley, Teunissen, & Montenbruck, 2017).

GNSS consists of three main components. These components are presented in Figure 6.1.

Satellite Positioning: Satellites in the GNSS system continuously transmit signals over the Earth's surface. These signals are received by the device to determine the user's position.

Receivers are devices that receive and process GNSS satellite signals. These receivers can be a variety of devices such as portable navigation devices, smartphones, and onboard navigation systems in vehicles.

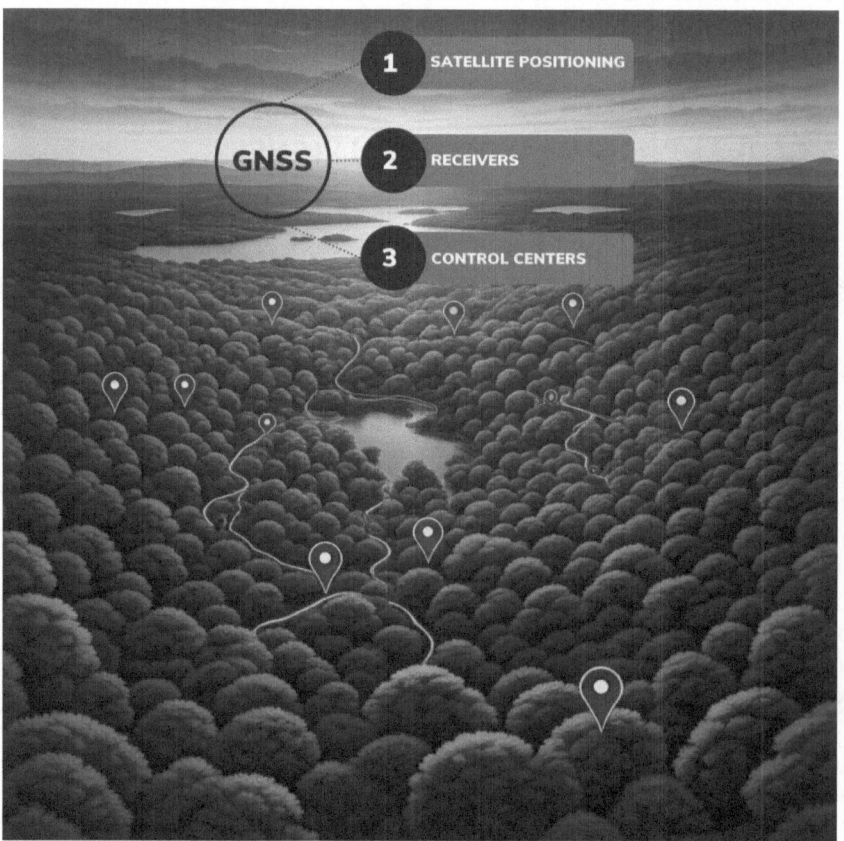

Figure 6.1 Main components of GNSS

Control Centers: These are the centers that manage GNSS systems and monitor satellite orbits and clock synchronization. These centers continuously monitor the systems and make corrections to ensure the accuracy of satellite signals.

The GNSS system allows the user to obtain accurate position information by receiving signals between the receiver and at least four satellites. The position is determined by calculating the reception time of these signals and the distances between the satellite and the receiver. GNSS receivers use complex algorithms to process multiple satellite signals simultaneously to determine the position even more precisely.

GNSS technology helps us in many aspects of our lives every day. It is used in many areas such as navigation, mapping, route planning, emergency management, and geographic data collection. It also plays an important role in finance, communications, and scientific research, ensuring accurate time synchronization.

GNSS technology is constantly evolving and being improved. New generation GNSS systems are being used more effectively in a variety of fields, offering higher precision, reliability, and availability. The expected future features of GNSS technology are presented in Figure 6.2.

Multiple Satellite Systems: In addition to existing GNSS systems, a new generation of satellite systems is being deployed. For example, the European Union's Galileo and China's Beidou work in conjunction with GPS and GLONASS to provide more satellites and better signal strength. A consolidated feedback has been prepared for the next generation of navigation satellite systems such as Galileo, GPS, and GLONASS, based on relevant experience in delivering products with the highest levels of accuracy from existing systems (Dow et al., 2007).

Galileo and Compass overlap in some regions of their signal frequencies, while GLONASS signals use more than 11 MHz of nearby bandwidth. Even bands that have not been used so far will be shared by many systems in the future (Hein et al., 2007).

Improved Precision: High precision is especially important in areas such as precision agriculture, construction, research, and air navigation. GNSS receivers and control centers are working to provide more precise position determination with advanced algorithms and corrections.

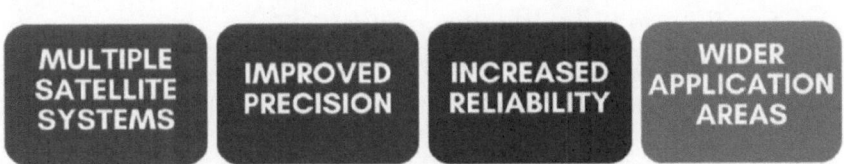

Figure 6.2 Expected future characteristics of GNSS technology

Increased Reliability: GPS studies benefit researchers by providing more accurate and reliable information about times, geographic locations, and routes (Schuessler & Axhausen, 2009).

GNSS signals can be interfered with or misleading in some cases. Therefore, various solutions are being studied to improve the reliability of GNSS systems. Especially in self-defense and military applications, anti-jamming and anti-spoofing technologies are important.

Wider Application Areas: The uses of GNSS technology continue to expand. For example, the role of GNSS is increasing in drone navigation, the development of autonomous vehicles and driverless vehicles, sports and health tracking systems, security applications, and industrial processes.

Thanks to these advances in GNSS technology, we are likely to see more accurate and reliable positioning systems and applications in the future. This will increase efficiency in many sectors and make our daily lives easier.

6.3 ELECTRO-OPTICAL AND LASER SYSTEMS

Electro-optical technologies refer to the integration of electrical energy with optical systems. These technologies use a combination of electromagnetic fields and optical materials to control, detect, transmit, and manipulate light. Electro-optical systems can be designed for use in a variety of applications and play an important role in many industrial, military, medical, and scientific fields.

The main components of electro-optical technologies are presented in Figure 6.3.

Electro-optical Crystals and Materials: Such crystals and materials interact with light and change their optical properties when exposed to electric fields. In this way, they can be used to focus, polarize, manipulate, and modulate light.

Photo Diodes and Photo Transistors: Photo diodes and photo transistors are electro-optical sensors that convert light into electrical signals. These

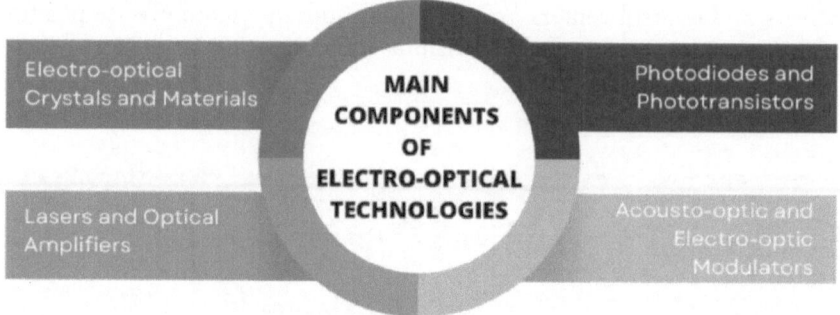

Figure 6.3 Main components of electro-optical technologies

components are used in light sensors, image sensors, and communication systems.

Lasers and Optical Amplifiers: Lasers are an important part of electro-optical technologies. They produce coherent light by exciting laser beams with electrical energy. Optical amplifiers are used to amplify optical signals and are widely used in optical fiber communications and scientific research.

Acousto-optic and Electro-optic Modulators: Acousto-optic modulators convert sound waves into optical signals, while electro-optic modulators convert electric fields into optical signals. These modulators are used in communication and processing applications by modulating signals.

Electro-optical technologies are used in applications as diverse as medical imaging, military reconnaissance and surveillance, laser processing, communications, space science, holography, and industrial sensors. These technologies are constantly being improved and are being actively studied by researchers to provide new application areas and higher performance. The application areas of electro-optical systems are presented in Figure 6.4.

Military Reconnaissance and Surveillance: Electro-optical technologies play an important role in military reconnaissance and surveillance systems. Satellite-based and aircraft-based electro-optical sensors are used to detect enemy activities, identify targets, collect geographic data, and provide visual intelligence. Electro-optical cameras can be equipped with features such as thermal imaging, night vision capabilities, and they can operate in different environments, increasing the effectiveness of military operations.

Laser Technologies: Lasers are an important part of electro-optical technologies and are used in many fields. Laser beams are high-intensity, coherent light sources and have applications ranging from communications, processing, and cutting to medical treatment and space exploration. A few areas where lasers are used include fiber optic communications, laser marking and cutting, laser surgery, and space observation.

Communication electro-optical technologies play an important role in the field of communication. A fiber optic communication system is used for high-speed and high-capacity data transmission. Components such as electro-optic modulators and optical amplifiers are used to modulate and amplify optical signals. Optical communication provides fast and reliable communication over long distances and is widely used in internet, telephone, and other communication networks.

Space Science: Space science has many applications for electro-optical technologies. Electro-optical cameras and telescopes are used for space

Figure 6.4 Areas of use of electro-optical systems

observation. In space exploration, electro-optical spectrometers and imaging devices are used to study the properties of stars and other space objects. Lasers also play an important role in the development of communication systems that can be used to transfer information and data in space.

Electro-optical technologies are a versatile and evolving field of technology, making significant contributions in military, industrial, and scientific fields. With new discoveries and advances constantly being made, the applications and effectiveness of these technologies will continue to expand.

In terms of weapon systems, electro-optical technologies play a critical role in improving the performance and targeting accuracy of modern weapons. Electro-optical technologies are used in surveillance, aiming, target acquisition, and firing phases of weapon platforms. Examples of the use of electro-optical technologies in weapon systems are presented in Figure 6.5.

Weapon Sights: Electro-optical sights provide precision aiming for rifles, sniper rifles, and other weapon systems. Optical sights can be equipped with electro-optical sensors such as laser rangefinders, thermal cameras, and night vision devices. This gives weapon users the ability to aim accurately and precisely at targets in both day and night conditions.

Laser Target Marking and Guidance: Electro-optical laser designators are used in guided munitions systems. These devices send a laser signal directly to the target, allowing the munition to be guided to the target. Laser-guided missiles are used for precision strikes and make it possible to hit targets with higher accuracy.

Weapon Systems Integration: Electro-optical technologies can be integrated into different weapon platforms such as tanks, warships, and fighter jets. With this integration, weapon systems have more effective target detection and attack capabilities. Electro-optical sensors enable weapon systems to continuously monitor their environment and detect threats.

Munition Detection and Realization: Electro-optical technologies enable accurate detection and realization of munitions. Electro-optical sensors are used to measure the munition's flight path and distance to its target. In addition, some munition systems can be equipped with thermal cameras that assess the temperature and reflectance characteristics of the target.

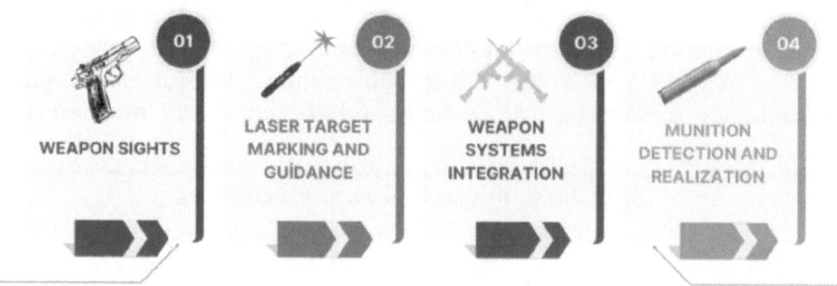

Figure 6.5 Electro-optical technologies in terms of weapon systems

Electro-optical technologies significantly impact the success of military operations by increasing the reliability, accuracy, and effectiveness of weapon systems. Modern weapon systems operate with greater precision, speed, and power by utilizing electro-optical advances in military technology. However, the use of these technologies must be balanced with principles of proper and ethical use, and appropriate precautions must be taken to avoid harm to civilians.

6.4 5G COMMUNICATION TECHNOLOGIES

5G technology is referred to as the fifth generation of wireless communications technology and improves on the previous generation of 4G technology. As 5G technology will not be able to meet the demands of the massive data traffic growth from massively interconnected devices projected in the coming years, the attention of the research community is shifting towards what the next innovations in wireless communication architectures and technologies will be (Qian, 2022).

5G is a significant step forward in mobile communications, offering a range of advanced features such as faster speeds, lower latency, and the ability to connect more devices simultaneously. The main features of 5G technology are presented in Figure 6.6.

Figure 6.6 Main features of 5G technology

High Data Rates: 5G provides a huge increase in download and upload speeds. Theoretically, 5G speeds can be up to 20 Gbps, giving users the ability to download and upload data much faster.

Low Latency: 5G significantly reduces communication latency. Theoretically, 5G latencies could be around 1 ms. These low latencies enable the development of real-time applications and services such as autonomous vehicles and virtual reality/augmented reality.

High Capacity: 5G enables more devices to connect simultaneously, delivering high performance even in densely populated areas. This makes it possible for more devices to stay connected in areas such as smart home devices, smart city applications, and industrial IoT (Internet of Things).

Better Coverage: 5G networks can cover a wider area using more antennas and provide better indoor coverage. This allows users to experience high-quality connectivity even indoors and in urban areas.

New Applications: 5G technology supports the development of next-generation applications such as virtual reality, augmented reality, remote surgery, smart cities, smart agriculture, and factory automation.

However, there are also some concerns with 5G technology. In particular, electromagnetic radiation and safety issues have been the subject of debate among some segments of the public. Therefore, it is important to consider such issues in the process of 5G deployment and utilization.

As a result, 5G technology is an important step towards a faster, more reliable, and more connected world. The 5G network is designed to have a wide range of applications and represents a major transformation in mobile communications. The working areas of 5G technology are presented in Figure 6.7.

5G Operating Frequencies: 5G technology operates in various frequency ranges. When the frequency bands to be used for 5G systems are examined, it is seen that they are divided into three separate sections: Low band, mid band, and high band. The low band is below 1 GHz, the mid band covers the frequency range of 1 GHz–6 GHz, and the high band covers the frequency band above 24 GHz (Türer & Yılmaz, 2022). Low frequencies provide wider coverage and better penetration into buildings, while

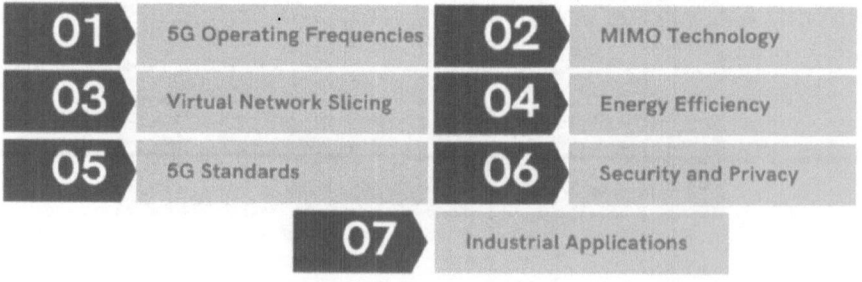

Figure 6.7 Working areas of 5G technology

high frequencies offer higher speeds and capacity but have more limited coverage.

MIMO Technology: Another technology that provides significant performance in wireless communication technology with 5G is dense MIMO. Dense MIMO is a technique in which a base station with hundreds of antenna arrays provides independent data flow to a large number of user terminals, each with a single antenna, at the same time or frequency range (Türer & Yılmaz, 2022).MIMO provides higher data rates and better connection quality.

Virtual Network Slicing: 5G offers a feature called virtual network slicing. This means that the network can be divided for different services. For example, different applications such as smart cities, smart factories, and autonomous vehicles can be offered customized and optimized networks.

Energy Efficiency: 5G technology is more energy efficient compared to previous generations of wireless technologies. This allows devices to have longer battery life and create a more sustainable network infrastructure. Large antenna arrays, coherent combining, and increased antenna aperture can potentially reduce user-base line (uplink) and base-user line (downlink) transmission powers. This method makes the transmit power of the user terminals inversely proportional to the number of antennas at the base station, so that the transmit power of the users decreases despite the increased number of base station antennas. As a result, Dense MIMO technology provides energy efficiency without any degradation in performance (Türer & Yılmaz, 2022).

5G Standards: Standards have been set for 5G technology to become widespread and work harmoniously. Organizations such as the International Telecommunication Union (ITU) and the third Generation Partnership Project (3GPP) lead the development and harmonized implementation of 5G standards.

Security and Privacy: The security and user privacy of 5G networks are of paramount importance. Measures should be taken to encrypt data, strengthen authentication methods, and detect and fix security vulnerabilities.

Industrial Applications: The next generation of 5G mobile networks is expected to enable the delivery of large-scale devices and new services (Akpakwu et al., 2017).

5G technology is having a major impact on industrial applications such as smart factories, the Internet of Things (IoT), autonomous vehicles, and healthcare. Industrial IoT enables real-time data sharing and interaction between machines and devices.

5G technology is considered a revolutionary advance in mobile communications, accelerating digital transformation processes and opening up new possibilities for applications across many industries. It enables the integration of the internet with a wider range of devices and services, and fast, reliable, and low latency connections, laying the foundations for the future digital society.

At the moment, there is no clear technology that will completely replace 5G. However, some future technological developments are being developed to build on or integrate with 5G. The technologies that could potentially replace or co-evolve with 5G are presented in Figure 6.8.

6G Technology: Work continues on 6G as the next-generation wireless communication technology on top of 5G. 6G technology will include features such as higher speeds, low latency, and greater device capacity. This technology is being developed to meet the demand for more data and speed in areas such as smart cities, medical applications, autonomous vehicles, and industrial IoT.

Future Communication Frequencies: Beyond 5G, wireless communication technologies operating in different frequency ranges will continue to be developed. In particular, technologies operating at terahertz frequencies may offer higher data rates and capacities, but this frequency range may also have more limited coverage.

Optical Communication and Fiber: Optical communication enables high-speed data transmission using fiber optic infrastructures. While this technology is not a full replacement for 5G, it can be used in some applications to provide higher data rates and reliable connections.

Artificial Intelligence and Edge Computing: AI and edge computing technologies contribute to making devices smarter and more data-driven. These technologies can be combined with 5G technology to optimize network traffic, process data faster, and enhance the user experience, creating smarter, data-driven networks.

Satellite Communications and Global Networks: Satellite communications can complement mobile communications technologies by providing

Figure 6.8 Technologies that may replace or coevolve with 5G

worldwide coverage. In the future, satellite communications and global networks can be combined with 5G technology to provide high-speed and reliable connections even in more remote areas.

As a result, while the exact technology that will replace 5G has not yet been determined, a more advanced communication network is expected to emerge in the future with the combination of technologies such as wireless communication, fiber optic infrastructure, and artificial intelligence. These technologies will play an important role in creating a smarter and more connected world by offering faster speeds, lower latency, and more capacity.

6.5 TECHNOLOGY TRENDS 2024–2050 AND REVOLUTIONARY TECHNOLOGIES FROM NATO'S PERSPECTIVE

Technology has been changing at an ever-increasing pace in recent years. Especially with the development of chip manufacturing technologies, significant developments have been achieved in hardware areas that require high processing power. These hardware advances have also caused software technologies to leap in scale.

Virtual Lives and Life Extension: Biological chip systems that can be implanted into the human nervous system or body can be developed with virtual universes created in digital environments. Depending on advances in biological research, developments such as longer use of the body and the continuation of life in digital spaces can be seen. An example of the use of virtual technology is presented in Figure 6.9.

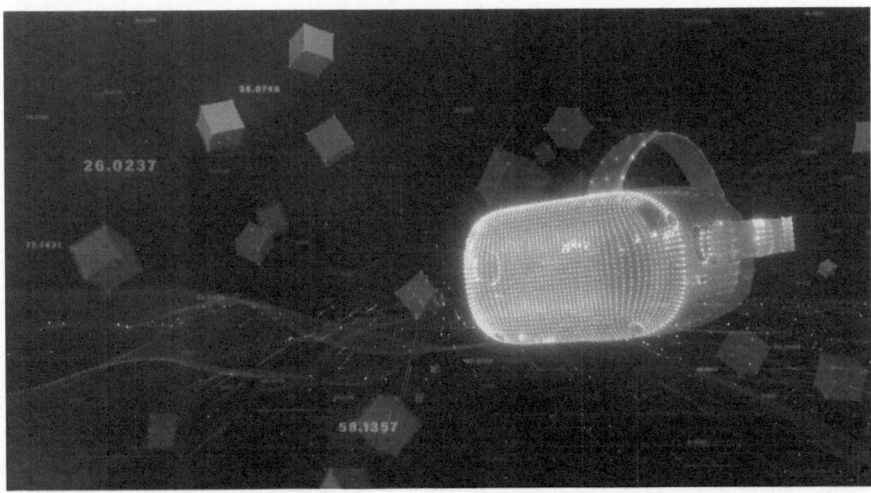

Figure 6.9 Use of virtual technology

Space Technologies and Space Exploration: Technologies for imaging distant galaxies could be further developed in areas such as long-duration space travel and interplanetary transportation. Space exploration and manned space flights could also become more common. An example of the Earth from inside a spacecraft is shown in Figure 6.10.

Clean Energy and Sustainable Technologies: Towards the 2040s, the adoption of clean and sustainable technologies in the energy sector and the increasing use of renewable energy sources are expected. With the use of more efficient renewable energy sources, all our energy sources can change. An example of wind turbines is presented in Figure 6.11.

Biotechnology and Health Technologies: Advances in biotechnology could support the development of new treatments and personalized medicine in the healthcare sector. Genes that are seen as defects in human DNA may be replaced.

Internet of Things (IoT) and Big Data Analytics: The Internet of Things (IoT) and big data analytics can be leveraged to increase efficiency in industries and improve the quality of life in areas such as smart cities. The use of wearable technologies may increase due to physiological measurement needs.

North Atlantic Treaty Organization (NATO) is a military and political alliance that has played an important role in international security and defense since the Cold War. Technological advancements have been one of the most important factors affecting the international security environment today.

NATO closely monitors the use of revolutionary technologies in defense and encourages their use to enhance the security capabilities of its member states (Reding & Eaton, 2020).

Figure 6.10 Earth from inside a spacecraft

Figure 6.11 Wind turbine

Artificial Intelligence and Autonomous Systems: Artificial intelligence is a technology that has the potential to revolutionize the military. Autonomous systems are rapidly developing in areas such as unmanned aerial vehicles (UAVs), unmanned maritime vehicles (UUVs), and unmanned ground vehicles (UGVs). These systems can be used in various missions such as reconnaissance, surveillance, intelligence, offence, and logistics.

Hybrid Warfare Technologies: The concept of hybrid warfare refers to the combination of traditional military operations with cyber attacks, information operations, and other asymmetric methods. These technologies involve the use of complex and diverse methods to neutralize the enemy.

Space and Space Security: Space is becoming increasingly important for military and civilian activities. The use of space technologies is increasing in areas such as satellite-based communications, reconnaissance, and intelligence. Space security involves the protection of strategically important space assets.

Electromagnetic Warfare: The electromagnetic spectrum has become a vital area for military operations. Electronic warfare and electromagnetic weapons are important technologies that can neutralize the enemy's communication, radar, and other electronic systems.

Hypersonic Technologies: Hypersonic technologies refer to high-speed and maneuverable systems such as hypersonic missiles and aircraft. These technologies are important for overcoming enemy air defenses and providing effective offensive capabilities.

Biotechnology and Chemical, Biological, Radiological, Nuclear (CBRN) Defense: Developments in the field of biotechnology offer new opportunities in combating biological threats. CBRN defense capabilities are essential to minimize the impact of attacks and protect public health.

NATO encourages the use of these revolutionary technologies to enhance the defense capabilities of member states and helps them adopt them safely. At the same time, NATO is exploring ways of cooperation and dialog to mitigate the negative impact of these technologies on international security and stability. Technological advances are an important factor constantly changing the international security environment and transforming defense strategies. NATO continues to promote the effective use of these revolutionary technologies to strengthen the defense capabilities of member states and ensure security.

Military security technologies have continuously evolved over the centuries in response to the threats facing humanity. Today, unique and pioneering technological solutions are being developed to enable military units to successfully accomplish their missions and gain the upper hand against enemy threats.

Advanced Weapon Systems: The most important element of military security is advanced weapon systems and missiles. Ballistic missiles, cruise missiles, and air defense systems increase the power of military units with their ability to neutralize threats and strike enemy targets with precision.

Intelligence and Reconnaissance Technologies: Intelligence gathering and reconnaissance technologies are vital for providing military units with advanced information and detecting enemy activities. Systems such as satellite imaging, unmanned aerial vehicles, and spy satellites enable the monitoring and analysis of enemy movements.

Electronic Warfare Systems: Electronic warfare systems have the ability to disrupt or neutralize the enemy's communication networks, radars, and electronic devices. This is used to weaken the enemy's ability to attack and increase the security of its own units.

Armor Technologies: Armor technologies are constantly being developed to protect military personnel and vehicles. Nano-armor, explosive reactive armor, and ballistic armor systems are used to protect personnel against bullets, shrapnel, and other threats.

Biometric Security: Biometric technologies are used for personnel authentication and access control. Methods such as fingerprint recognition, facial recognition, and retinal scanning are effective in securing sensitive military installations.

Cyber Security: Another important element of military security in the digital age is cyber security. Resilient networks and security software prevent enemies from infiltrating computer systems, ensuring the security of important data and communications.

In conclusion, military security technologies are vital for ensuring superiority on the modern battlefield and the safety of personnel. These continuously evolving technologies contribute to global security by strengthening the defense capability of nations. However, the use of these technologies should be controlled by ethical and legal regulations. This encourages their use for peaceful purposes and prevents their misuse.

REFERENCES

Akpakwu, G. A., Silva, B. J., Hancke, G. P., & Abu-Mahfouz, A. M. (2017). A survey on 5G networks for the internet of things: Communication technologies and challenges. *IEEE Access*, 6, 3619–3647.

Dow, J. M., Neilan, R. E., Weber, R., & Gendt, G. (2007). Galileo and the IGS: Taking advantage of multiple GNSS constellations. *Advances in Space Research*, 39(10), 1545–1551.

Hein, G. W., Rodriguez, J., Wallner, S., Eissfeller, B., Pany, T. H. O. M. A. S., & Hartl, P. (2007). Envisioning a future GNSS system of systems. *Inside GNSS*, 2(1), 58–67.

Langley, R. B., Teunissen, P. J., & Montenbruck, O. (2017). Introduction to GNSS. Springer handbook of global navigation satellite systems, 3–23.

McNeff, J. G. (2002). The global positioning system. *IEEE Transactions on Microwave Theory and Techniques*, 50(3), 645–652.

Qian, Y. (2022). Beyond 5G wireless communication technologies. *IEEE Wireless Communications*, 29(1), 2–3.

Reding, D. F., & Eaton, J. (2020). Science & technology trends 2020–2040. Exploring the S&T edge. NATO science & technology organization, 71–73.

Schuessler, N., & Axhausen, K. W. (2009). Processing raw data from global positioning systems without additional information. *Transportation Research Record*, 2105(1), 28–36.

Türer, B., & Yılmaz, M. (2022). New technologies in 5G cellular communication systems. *European Journal of Science and Technology*, 36, 128–133.